THE BOOK OF NERO 6 ULTRA EDITION

CD and DVD Burning Made Easy

by Wallace Wang

NO STARCH
PRESS

San Francisco

Publisher: William Pollock
Managing Editor: Karol Jurado
Developmental Editor: William Pollock
Cover and Interior Design: Octopod Studios
Technical Reviewer: Ahead Software
Copyeditor: Andy Carroll
Compositor: Wedobooks
Proofreader: Stephanie Provines
Indexer: Kevin Broccoli

For information on book distributors or translations, please contact No Starch Press, Inc. directly:

No Starch Press, Inc.
555 De Haro Street, Suite 250, San Francisco, CA 94107
phone: 415-863-9900; fax: 415-863-9950; info@nostarch.com; http://www.nostarch.com

Library of Congress Cataloguing-in-Publication Data

Wang, Wallace.
  The book of Nero 6 Ultra Edition : CD and DVD burning made easy / Wallace Wang.
      p. cm.
  Includes index.
  ISBN 1-59327-043-7
  1. Nero (Electronic resource) 2. CD-Rs. 3. DVD-ROMs. 4. Sound--Recording and reproducing.
I. Title.
  TK7895.C39W36 2004
  004.5'65--dc22
                                                                                    2004007852

THE BOOK OF
NERO 6 ULTRA EDITION

DEDICATION

This book is dedicated to all the people who have helped me along the way through the chaotic world of stand-up comedy:

All the friendly folks I've met at the Riviera Comedy Club, located at the Riviera Hotel & Casino (www.rivierahotel.com) in Las Vegas: Steve Schirripa (who appears in HBO's hit show, *The Sopranos*), Bob Zany (www.bobzany.com) Gerry Bednob, Bruce Clark, Darrell Joyce, Tony Vicich, and Kip Addotta.

Additional thanks go to Joe Jarred, who books wonderful little comedy shows in Pahrump and Primm, Nevada, two places that you will probably never see listed anywhere in a tourist guide; Don Learned at the Laff Spot in Houston (www.laffspot.com); Roger Feeny at the Ann Arbor Comedy Showcase (www.aacomedy.com); Connie Ettinger at the Holly Hotel Comedy Club (www.hollyhotel.com); Doug James for his wonderful little one-nighters all over Southern California; and Mark Ridley at the Comedy Castle (www.comedycastle.com).

Patrick DeGuire also deserves thanks, not because he helped with this book (he didn't) but because he helped me form Top Bananas Entertainment (www.topbananas.com) — our company devoted to providing clean, quality stand-up comedy for the wonderful people in San Diego. Additional thanks must also go to Chris (the Zooman) Clobber, Dante, Dobie "Mr. Lucky" Maxwell, and Leo (the man, the myth, the legend) Fontaine just because they like seeing their names in print for no apparent reason.

Continuing the theme of thanking people who had nothing to do with this book, the author would also like to dedicate this book to LeStat's (www.lestats.com), the best little coffeehouse in San Diego, for providing a warm, friendly environment to practice stand-up comedy in the safety and comfort of intelligent people who haven't drowned their inhibitions (and intelligence) away into an alcoholic stupor.

Final thanks go to Cassandra (my wife), Jordan (my son) and Bo, Scraps, Tasha, and Nuit (our cats) for making my life more interesting by the minute.

BRIEF CONTENTS

CONTENTS IN DETAIL

INTRODUCING NERO

1
GETTING STARTED WITH THE STARTSMART MENU

2
SAVING MUSIC ON A CD

3

STORING AND BACKING UP DATA

4

SAVING PHOTOS AS A SLIDE SHOW

5
BURNING A VIDEO DISC

6
DESIGNING CD AND DVD LABELS AND COVERS

7
EDITING SOUND

8

PLAYING AUDIO

9

PLAYING VIDEO

10
RECORDING AUDIO FROM LPs AND TAPES

11
CAPTURING AND EDITING VIDEO

12
USING THE NERO TOOLKIT

A
INSTALLING, UPDATING, AND UNINSTALLING NERO

INDEX
187

ACKNOWLEDGMENTS

Matt Wagner and Bill Gladstone at Waterside Productions deserve special acknowledgement because if they weren't my agents, I might actually have to deal with negotiating royalties from book publishers myself. These two guys are the best agents an author could hope for, so they deserve all the 15 percent of the book royalties that they get.

Some other people who deserve thanks include Bill Pollock and Karol Jurado for making No Starch Press one of the best little publishers in the entire universe of computer book publishers. Additional thanks go out to Ahead Software for making Nero and reviewing this book for technical accuracy.

A final note of thanks go to anyone who has actually read the Dedication and Acknowledgments pages because those pages usually contain useless information that nobody except the author and his closest friends even care about. Thanks for reading this — and say a prayer for all the trees that sacrificed their pulp to allow authors (such as myself) the indulgence to print paragraphs such as this.

Wally Wang
San Diego, CA

INTRODUCING NERO

For several years, Nero has earned a reputation for being one of the most powerful CD and DVD burning programs on the market. While Nero can help you create your own CDs and DVDs, you may be pleasantly surprised to know that Nero can do a whole lot more.

To make your CDs and DVDs look more professional, Nero can design labels that you can paste directly onto your discs, and disc covers that you can slip inside a plastic CD/DVD case. If you have music stored on old vinyl records or tape cassettes that you want to preserve, Nero can not only help you transfer them to a CD, but Nero can also help you edit the sound quality to eliminate any hisses or pops that might mar the original recording. With Nero's sound-editing capabilities, you can even make your record or tape recordings sound as if they had been stored on CD in the first place.

Nero also comes with its own audio and video players, so you can listen to CDs and watch full-length DVD movies on your computer. If you've captured your own home movies on video cassette or on a digital video camera, Nero can help you edit your video before burning it to a DVD.

Not only can Nero help you store, edit, and burn audio and video files to CDs and DVDs, but it can guide you through this process so you'll spend more time getting work done and less time trying to figure out how to do it.

What You Need to Get Started

Besides a copy of Nero 6, you also need a rewritable CD/DVD drive along with a stack of blank discs. While you're learning to use Nero to make your own CDs and DVDs, it's usually a good idea to have a handful of rewritable CDs and DVDs around so you can experiment saving data, music, or video on CD or DVD. That way, if you make a mistake with a rewritable CD or DVD, you can just erase the whole thing and start over. Once you have all of these items, you'll be ready to start saving data and storing your own audio and video files on CDs and DVDs with your very own computer.

How to Use This Book

If you're just getting started with Nero 6 and haven't even opened up the box yet, skip ahead to Appendix A to learn how to both install Nero 6 and update your copy to the latest version available. Because Nero 6 actually consists of several different programs, you may not want to install all of them. If you make a mistake or change your mind about something you've installed, see Appendix A to learn how to selectively uninstall some or all the different programs that come with Nero 6.

Once you get Nero installed and updated, you're ready to start back at the beginning of the book. Chapter 1 explains the easy way to find and run all of the different Nero programs installed on your computer.

Chapter 2 shows you how to create your own CDs to store your favorite music, whether you want to copy an entire audio CD or just a handful of songs. In case you have a bunch of audio files trapped in different file formats, such as MP3, this chapter will tell you how to store them on a CD too.

Because everyone has important data that they can't afford to lose, Chapter 3 tells you how to back up your valuable files to CDs or DVDs. With Nero's handy scheduling program, you can do this automatically, so you can concentrate on your work and let Nero and your computer worry about backing up your data.

If you're like many people, you may have a digital camera that you're using to capture all types of pictures that you may be storing on your hard disk. Although you could just print those pictures out and hand them to your friends, Chapter 4 will show you how to arrange and organize your digital pictures on a CD or DVD to create your own presentation slide shows for either personal or business use.

In Chapter 5, you can learn all about copying and making your own DVDs. While Nero won't let you copy any copy-protected DVDs, it will let you copy an entire DVD or just parts of one, so you can keep all the good parts without bothering to copy anything else that you don't want.

After you create a CD or DVD, you may not want to use a marker pen to scribble a title across the disc, so Chapter 6 shows you how Nero can help you design disc labels complete with text, color, and graphics. Besides designing labels, you can also use Nero to design covers for CD and DVD cases of all different sizes.

Sometimes music stored on a computer might not sound as crisp and clear as you might like, so Chapter 7 shows you how to use Nero to edit your audio files to adjust the volume or modify the way they sound.

Nero is more than just a CD/DVD creation program. In Chapter 8, you'll learn how Nero can also play your audio files, turning your personal computer into your stereo. In Chapter 9, you'll learn how to play full-length DVD movies and video files too, so you can turn your computer into both a CD and a DVD player.

If you grew up in the time before CDs became popular, you may have old recordings trapped on vinyl records, like mosquitoes trapped in amber. But unlike prehistoric mosquitoes, any music trapped on vinyl records can be captured on your computer, converted to an audio file, and saved on a CD. In Chapter 10, you'll learn step-by-step directions for converting your favorite records and tapes to audio files and bringing your record collection into the modern age.

Besides letting you edit audio files, Nero also lets you capture and edit video files that you can store on a DVD to pass around to your friends and relatives. If you're an aspiring filmmaker or just a video camera enthusiast, you'll want to read Chapter 11 to learn how to create your own videos.

Finally, Chapter 12 shows you how to use all of the diagnostic tools that come with Nero so you can check into your CD and DVD drive capabilities and even alter the way your rewritable CD or DVD drives work.

You could read this book from cover to cover, but it's more likely that you'll just need to learn how to use one part of Nero, so feel free to skip to the chapter that you want and ignore the rest of the book until you need it. With a copy of Nero 6 on your computer and the help of this book, you'll find that making your own CDs and DVDs will be faster and easier than you ever thought possible.

Conventions

To use Nero, you'll probably use your mouse, but occasionally you may want to use the keyboard as a faster alternative to the mouse. To give a command with the keyboard, you often have to press a combination of keys. So rather than tell you to press the **CTRL** key followed by the **A** key, this book uses the shortcut convention *Keystroke1+Keystroke2* such as *CTRL+A*.

Some other conventions you may see in this book relate to using the mouse. Most of the time when an instruction says to use the mouse to choose a command, that means you point the mouse to a command and then click the left mouse button. If you're supposed to click the right mouse button, this book will tell you to right-click, and if you're supposed to click the left mouse button, this book will tell you just to click.

Who Should Use This Book

Whether you're a seasoned computer veteran or a novice, you'll find something in this book for you. Nero is a powerful and versatile program, and beginners may find themselves overwhelmed at first. However, with a little patience and the help of this book, you'll find that Nero is a friendly, easy-to-use tool. And maybe your dream project of a home movie with a soundtrack pulled from your record collection isn't so far-fetched after all.

1

GETTING STARTED WITH THE STARTSMART MENU

Nero may be packaged as a single program, but it actually consists of several separate programs that work together. Nero's main program focuses on burning data to CD/DVD discs, but Nero's supplementary programs allow you to edit audio and video files and design CD/DVD labels as well. Unfortunately, with so many different programs available, knowing which Nero program to use for a particular task can be intimidating.

Fortunately, Nero provides a one-stop menu that gives you access to all the features available in all the different Nero programs. With the StartSmart menu, you can tell Nero what you want to do and let Nero worry about running the right program to help you do it.

Starting the StartSmart Menu

To use the StartSmart menu, you first must find it. Basically, there are two ways to load the StartSmart menu:

- Double-click the **StartSmart** icon on your desktop.
- Click the **Start** button, click **All Programs**, click **Nero**, and click **Nero StartSmart**.

When you do either of these, the Nero StartSmart menu will appear, as shown in Figure 1-1.

Figure 1-1: Nero's StartSmart menu lets you choose which task you want to do without needing to know which Nero program will actually do it

Putting the StartSmart Icon on Your Desktop

When you install Nero for the first time, it puts the NeroStartSmart icon on your desktop. However, if you can't find the StartSmart icon for any reason, you can add it to your desktop manually by following these steps:

1. Right-click your desktop (make sure you don't click over any icons). A pop-up menu appears.
2. Click **New**, and when another pop-up menu appears, click **Shortcut**. A Create Shortcut dialog box appears.
3. Click **Browse**. A Browse for Folder dialog box appears. Click the **My Computer** icon, click the **Local Disk (C:)** icon, click **Program Files**, click **Ahead**, click **Nero StartSmart**, and (finally) click the **NeroStartSmart** icon as shown in Figure 1-2.

NOTE   *If you installed Nero on a different drive or folder, you'll have to find the NeroStartSmart icon buried in the drive and folder where you initially installed the program.*

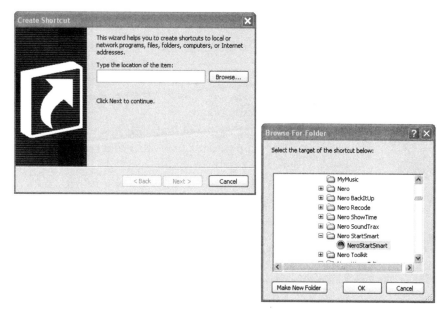

Figure 1-2: To put the NeroStartSmart icon on your desktop, you first have to find it buried somewhere on your hard disk

4. Click **OK** The Create Shortcut dialog box displays the StartSmart filename.
5. Click **Next**. The Select a Title for the Program dialog box appears and asks whether you want to change the name of your shortcut icon.
6. Click **Finish**. Your NeroStartSmart icon appears on your desktop.

Deleting the StartSmart Icon from Your Desktop

You can always delete the NeroStartSmart icon from your desktop at any time by following these steps:

1. Right-click the **NeroStartSmart** icon. A pop-up menu appears.
2. Click **Delete**. A dialog box appears, asking if you really want to delete your shortcut icon.
3. Click **Delete Shortcut**. The NeroStartSmart icon gets dumped in the Recycle Bin.

Using Nero from the StartSmart Menu

The whole purpose of the StartSmart menu is to help you find and run one of the many Nero programs. Although the StartSmart menu may seem confusing with its multiple options, commands, and icons to choose from, relax. To use the most common commands in the StartSmart menu, you just need to figure out the following:

1. What type of data you want to save (audio, video, or data)?

    Audio files   This includes MP3, WAV, and other files that only contain sound.

    Video and digital photograph files   This includes JPEG, Quick-Time, and other types of files that contain still or moving images plus sound.

    Data files   This includes any type of data, such as word processor documents, database files, spreadsheet files, and so on.

2. Where you want to save it (on a CD or a DVD)?

Choosing a Category

Once you know what type of data you want to save, you need to select a command to save your particular type of files. To help you out, the StartSmart menu organizes commands for saving specific types of files into one of six different categories, as shown in Figure 1-3:

Figure 1-3: There are six categories where you can find commands for saving different types of data to a CD or DVD

- **Favorites**   Lists your most commonly used commands
- **Data**   Stores files on a CD or DVD to transfer them to another computer
- **Audio**   Saves music on a CD or DVD
- **Photo and video**   Saves digital photographs and video files on a CD or DVD
- **Copy and backup**   Copies files off a hard disk or restores files from a CD or DVD
- **Extras**   Lists miscellaneous commands for working with CD or DVD discs, such as erasing discs, testing a CD or DVD drive, or making a CD or DVD label

Each time you click a category, the StartSmart menu displays a list of commands to choose from. So if you click the Audio category, the StartSmart menu displays different commands for saving audio files on a CD or DVD.

Choosing Your Disc Type

Once you know what type of files you want to save, the next step is choosing to save them to a CD or DVD. To tell the StartSmart menu what type of disc to use, click the CD or DVD tab, as shown in Figure 1-4. (If you only have a CD drive, you won't see any options for saving anything to a DVD.)

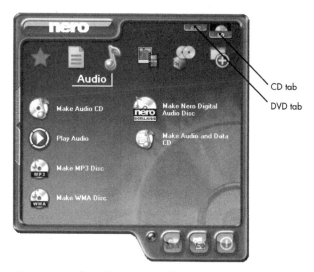

Figure 1-4: Before choosing a task, you must tell the Nero StartSmart menu which type of disc you want to use, a CD or DVD

Depending on whether you chose to use a CD or DVD, the StartSmart menu displays slightly different options, as shown in Figures 1-5 and 1-6 .

Figure 1-5: Options for saving files to a CD

Figure 1-6: Options for saving files to a DVD

Choosing a Command

Once you've chosen a category (such as audio or data) and specified what type of disc to save it to (CD or DVD), all you have to do next is click the particular command you want, such as **Make Audio CD** or **Back up Files**.

(You may need to switch from standard mode to expert mode to find the command you want, as described in the next section.)

As soon as you choose a command, the StartSmart menu loads the Nero program you need. When you exit from that Nero program, the StartSmart menu pops up again.

NOTE *You'll learn more about using the specific Nero programs later in the book. For now, it's just important that you understand that the StartSmart menu will help you find the right Nero program to use, based on what you want to do.*

Switching Between Standard and Expert Modes

If you want to copy music files to a CD that you can play in an ordinary stereo, the StartSmart menu can simplify that task through its point-and-click interface. However, if you want to do something more advanced, like making a bootable CD or ripping music off an audio CD, then you may not find those particular commands on the StartSmart menu unless you first switch to expert mode.

Standard mode (shown in Figure 1-7) just lists the most commonly used commands within a category, but expert mode (shown in Figure 1-8 on the next page) offers additional commands for saving files to a CD or DVD.

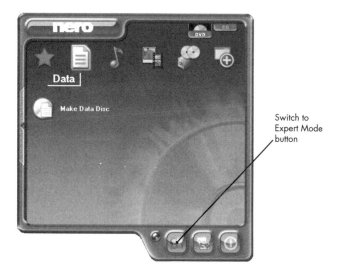

Switch to
Expert Mode
button

Figure 1-7: Standard mode lists the most common commands you may want to choose

To switch between standard and expert modes, just click the **Standard Mode** or **Expert Mode** button.

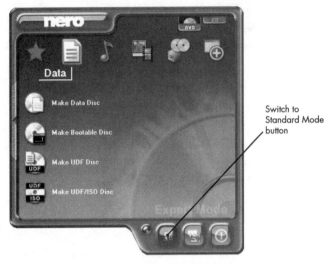

Switch to
Standard Mode
button

Figure 1-8: Expert mode lists every possible command available within a category

Running a Program Through the StartSmart Menu

The StartSmart menu shields you from having to choose which specific Nero program you want to run. However, you can still run a particular Nero program through the StartSmart menu if you want.

To run a specific program, follow these steps:

1. Start the StartSmart menu.
2. Click the **StartSmart bar** to display a menu that offers three choices: Applications, Nero Toolkit, and Manuals, as shown in Figure 1-9.

StartSmart
bar

Figure 1-9: Clicking the StartSmart bar displays a menu

Applications   Displays a list of different Nero CD and DVD burning programs

Nero Toolkit   Displays a list of diagnostic tools

Manuals   Displays the user manual for a particular Nero program in Adobe Acrobat format

3. Click **Applications** or **Nero Toolkit**. A menu of additional programs appears, as shown in Figure 1-10.

Figure 1-10: If you click Applications, the StartSmart menu displays a list of individual Nero programs you can run

4. Click a program name, such as **Nero Express**, and the StartSmart menu loads your chosen program. When you exit from this program, the StartSmart menu pops back up on the screen again.

5. Click the **StartSmart bar** to hide the Applications, Nero Toolkit, and Manuals menu from view.

Customizing StartSmart

Most people only use a handful of Nero's features, but no two people use the exact same ones. Nero offers many features so that everyone can choose the ones they want to use.

Customizing the Favorites Category

Although the StartSmart menu doesn't know which features you find most useful, you can customize the Favorites category to store all your commonly used commands.

To store a command in the Favorites category, follow these steps:

1. Start the Nero StartSmart menu.

2. Click a category such as **Data** or **Audio**. The StartSmart menu displays a list of commands. (To see all available commands, click the **Expert Mode** button.)

3. Right-click a command that you want to store in your Favorites category. A pop-up menu appears, as shown in Figure 1-11.

4. Click **Add to Favorites**. Nero immediately copies your chosen command to the Favorites category.

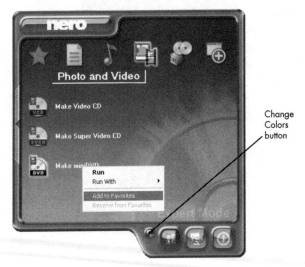

Figure 1-11: Right-click a command to copy it to the Favorites category

The Favorites category can be handy for finding the commands you want to use right away. However, you may eventually find that you don't use some commands as often as you had thought you might. Rather than let these seldom-used commands clutter up your Favorites category, you can remove them by following these steps:

1. Start the Nero StartSmart menu.

2. Click the **Favorites** category to see a list of your commonly used commands.

3. Right-click a command that you want to delete. A pop-up menu appears.

4. Click **Remove from Favorites**. Nero immediately removes your chosen command from the Favorites category.

Changing Colors

If you don't like the colors used to display the StartSmart menu, you can always change them by clicking the **Change Colors** button (see Figure 1-11). Changing colors doesn't affect the way the StartSmart menu works; it's purely for your own visual pleasure.

Minimizing and Quitting StartSmart

No matter how useful you find the Nero StartSmart menu, eventually you will want to get it out of sight. If you think you may want to use the Nero StartSmart menu again, you can minimize it. If you want to shut it down completely, you can quit it, which removes it from memory.

Minimizing the StartSmart Menu

When you minimize the StartSmart menu, you just tuck it out of sight, but it still runs in memory. To minimize the StartSmart menu, follow these steps:

1. Right-click the **NeroStartSmart** icon on the Windows taskbar. A pop-up menu appears.
2. Click **Minimize**. Windows tucks the Nero StartSmart menu out of sight and displays its icon on the Windows taskbar. To open the Nero StartSmart menu again, just click the **NeroStartSmart** icon in the Windows taskbar.

Quitting the StartSmart Menu

If you want to shut down the Nero StartSmart menu, you have three options:

- Click anywhere on the Nero StartSmart menu, and then press **ALT+F4**.
- Click the **Exit** button at the bottom-right corner of the Nero StartSmart menu, as shown in Figure 1-12 on the next page.
- Right-click the **Nero StartSmart** icon on the Windows taskbar, and when a pop-up menu appears, click **Close**, as shown in Figure 1-12 on the next page.

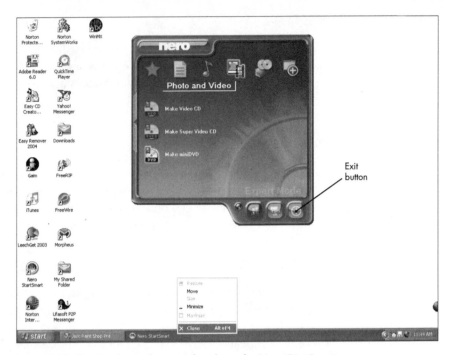

Figure 1-12: The Exit button lets you shut down the Nero StartSmart menu

In the next chapter, we'll work with audio CDs.

2

SAVING MUSIC ON A CD

One of the more popular uses for Nero is making audio CDs, either by duplicating an existing audio CD or by creating a custom audio CD (sometimes referred to as "burning a CD") that contains your own personal selection of audio tracks. For extra versatility, you can even create CDs that hold both audio files and ordinary data files. That way you can take your favorite music along with your important data wherever you have a CD drive and a computer.

Nero gives you three different ways to create an audio CD:

- Burn an audio CD with copies of audio tracks from another audio CD
- Burn a CD that contains both audio tracks and data files
- Burn an audio CD that contains digital audio files, such as MP3 files

There are two types of discs you can use to create an audio CD: CD-R and CD+RW. A CD-R disc is less expensive but can only be written to once. A CD+RW disc can be rewritten over and over again. You may want to experiment with CD+RW discs and when you save data correctly on a CD+RW disc, you can always transfer it to a CD-R disc later.

WARNING   *Legally, you may only copy audio CDs if you own the copyright or have written permission of the copyright owner. Illegally, you can do whatever you want just as long as you realize that you're ultimately responsible for your own actions.*

Copying an Entire Audio CD Quickly

If you have one drive that can read CDs and another drive that can write CDs, you can copy an entire audio CD from one drive to another, a process known as *on-the-fly copying.* (If your computer only has a single CD/DVD drive, you'll first have to copy audio tracks from the audio CD to your hard disk and then burn those audio tracks to a disc in a second step, as explained in the "Burning Selected Tracks from Audio CDs" section later in this chapter.)

NOTE   *The main drawback with on-the-fly copying is that if there are scratches on the original CD or if the speeds of your CD drive and your rewritable CD or DVD drive don't match, it's possible that Nero won't burn a copy of your CD correctly.*

Checking for Buffer Underrun Protection

One problem with on-the-fly copying is that you risk buffer underrun, which occurs when the CD or DVD drive doing the burning doesn't receive a continuous stream of data. So while your rewritable CD/DVD drive is waiting for more data to burn, it winds up burning nothing, essentially wrecking your copy of the CD.

To prevent buffer underruns, many rewritable CD and DVD drives offer built-in buffer underrun protection. To check whether your rewritable CD or DVD drive offers buffer underrun protection, follow these steps:

1. Load the StartSmart menu.
2. Click the **CD** tab in the upper-right corner of the StartSmart menu. (If your computer does not have a rewritable CD and DVD drive, the CD tab may not be visible.)
3. Click the **Extras** category.
4. Click **Get System Info**. The Nero InfoTool program runs and displays a dialog box that lists the capabilities of your rewritable CD or DVD drive, as shown in Figure 2-1. If your rewritable CD or DVD drive offers buffer underrun protection, you'll see a check mark in the Buffer Underrun Protection check box.

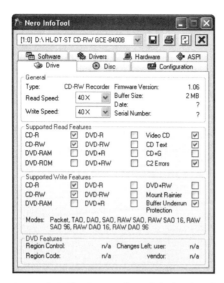

Figure 2-1: The Nero InfoTool dialog box lists the type of CD or DVD discs your rewritable drive can use, along with whether it offers buffer underrun protection

5. Click the **Exit** button or **Close** box to close the InfoTool dialog box. The StartSmart menu pops up again.

NOTE *If your rewritable CD or DVD drive does not offer buffer underrun protection, you'll have to manually adjust the burn speed of your rewritable drive, which you'll learn about in the next section.*

On-the-Fly Copying of an Audio CD

Once you've determined that your rewritable CD or DVD drive offers buffer underrun protection, you can make an exact duplicate of an audio CD through on-the-fly copying by following these steps:

1. Insert your audio CD in your CD or DVD drive.
2. Insert a blank CD-R or CD+RW disc in your CD or DVD rewritable drive. (If you insert a CD+RW disc that already has some data stored on it, Nero can erase it prior to burning your CD.)

NOTE *Many older CD players may not be able to play audio CDs recorded on CD-R or CD+RW discs.*

3. Start the StartSmart menu.
4. Click the **Audio** category.
5. Click the **Copy Disc** button. The Nero Express window appears, as shown in Figure 2-2 on the next page.

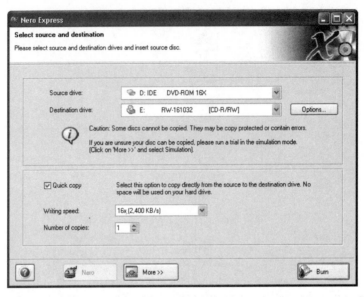

Figure 2-2: The Nero Express window lets you choose Quick copy (on-the-fly copying) and adjust the burn speed of your rewritable CD or DVD drive.

6. Make sure a check mark appears in the **Quick copy** check box. With the quick copy enabled, Nero will copy your audio CD directly to your recordable CD.

7. (Optional.) If your rewritable CD or DVD drive does not offer buffer underrun protection, click in the **Writing speed** list box and choose a writing speed that matches the access speed listed in the **Source drive** list box, such as **16x**.

NOTE *If you want to check whether Nero can successfully copy your CD, you can run a simulation. That way, if the simulation doesn't work, you won't have to wreck a recordable CD disc by burning a CD that won't copy correctly. To simulate burning a CD, click the More button and click the Simulation check box, as shown in Figure 2-3. Then in step 8, instead of clicking the Burn button, just click the Simulate button. If a check mark appears in both the Simulation and Write check boxes, Nero will first simulate the burning process, and if it works correctly, then it will start burning your CD automatically.*

8. Click the **Burn** button. Nero Express starts burning your copy of the audio CD. When your copy is done, Nero Express displays a window to inform you that the burn successfully completed, as shown in Figure 2-4.

9. Click **Next**. Nero Express ejects your audio CD and your copy and displays the Nero Express window.

10. Click **Exit**. The StartSmart menu appears again.

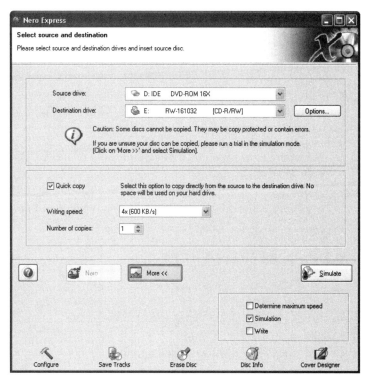

Figure 2-3: Nero can simulate burning a CD so you can test whether you can successfully copy a CD or not

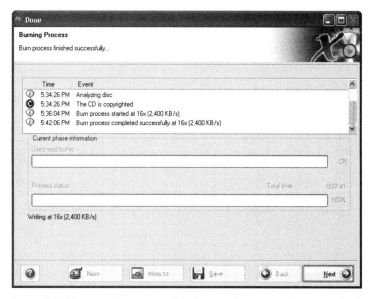

Figure 2-4: The Nero Express window lets you know when Nero has finished burning your copy of the audio CD

Burning Selected Tracks from Audio CDs

Often when you buy a commercial audio CD, you'll find a handful of songs that you like, and a lot of filler songs that you may not like. Rather than listen to songs you hate, take the time to make your own custom audio CD that strips away the lousy songs and just leaves you with the really good ones.

To burn your own compilation audio CD, you just need to follow these basic steps:

1. Select the audio tracks you want from one or more CDs and save them to your hard disk.
2. (Optional.) Modify the audio tracks by rearranging their order, renaming them, adjusting the volume of each track, and so on.
3. Burn your audio tracks on a CD.

Selecting Audio Tracks from a CD

To select audio tracks from an audio CD, follow these steps:

1. Insert an audio CD in your CD or DVD drive.
2. Start the StartSmart menu.
3. Click the **CD** tab in the upper-right corner of the StartSmart menu.
4. Click the **Audio** category.
5. Click **Make Audio CD**. The Nero Express window appears.
6. Click the **Add** button. A Select Files and Folders dialog box appears, as shown in Figure 2-5.

Figure 2-5: The Select Files and Folders dialog box lets you choose which audio tracks you want to burn

7. Click an audio track you want to select. To select more than one audio track, hold down the **CTRL** key and click the audio tracks you want to select. To select a range of audio tracks, click the first audio track you want to select, hold down the **SHIFT** key, and then click the last audio track you want to select. Nero Express selects those two audio tracks along with all the tracks sandwiched in between.

8. Click **Add**. The Nero's Title and CD Database window appears, asking whether you want to retrieve artist and title information from a database on the Internet.

9. Click **Yes** if you have an Internet connection, and when the Nero's Title and CD Database window appears, click the **Access Internet Database** button. Nero retrieves information about your CD, including the album and individual song titles, as shown in Figure 2-6. Then click the **Selected CD** button. Your chosen audio tracks appear in the Nero Express window.

   If you don't have an Internet connection and you click **No** for this step, an Enter Source CD Name dialog box appears, where you can type in the name of your CD. Type a name and click **OK**.

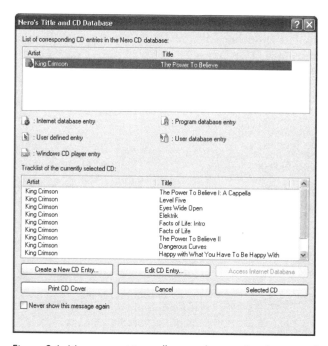

Figure 2-6: Nero can retrieve album and song title information from the Internet automatically

10. (Optional.) Insert another audio CD and repeat steps 6–9 to select tracks from a different audio CD.

11. (Optional.) If you want to delete an audio track from your list of selected tracks, click that audio track and then click **Delete**.

As you add audio tracks, Nero Express displays a blue horizontal bar at the bottom to show you how many minutes your audio tracks take up. Most CDs can hold approximately 74 minutes of audio tracks, so if you go over this limit, there's a chance that your last audio track may get cut off.

Modifying Audio Tracks

Once you've selected one or more audio tracks, you may want to take some time to modify the way the tracks will appear and sound by doing one of the following:

- Edit the title of the song
- Edit the name of the recording artist
- Specify the number of seconds of silence after each song
- Enable (or disable) copy protection
- Include cross-fades

To modify an audio track, make sure the Nero Express window is visible, and then follow these steps:

1. Click the audio track you want to modify.
2. Click the **Properties** button (or right-click an audio track and select **Properties**). The Audio Track Properties dialog box appears, as shown in Figure 2-7.

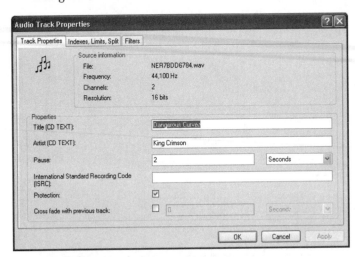

Figure 2-7: The Audio Track Properties dialog box lets you modify the title of each song and specify the length of pauses between songs

3. Make changes to one or more of the following settings:

   Title   Displays the song title when played on a computer or certain CD players.

   Artist   Displays the recording artist's name on a computer or certain CD players.

Pause   Specifies the amount of silence at the end of a song. Two seconds is normal, but for songs meant to be played right after another, change this value to 0.

Protection   Enables (or disables) copy protection so that the song can or cannot be copied.

Cross fade with previous track   Plays the end of one song so it overlaps the beginning of the following song.

4. Click **OK** when you're finished making changes to your song. The Nero Express window appears again.

5. Click the **Normalize all audio files** check box to set all audio tracks at the same volume. (This is only useful if you've copied audio tracks from two or more audio CDs.)

6. Click the **No pause between tracks** check box if you don't want any pauses between any of your audio tracks. (This will override any pause settings you may have specified in step 3.)

Rearranging Audio Tracks

Once you've selected your audio tracks and they appear in the Nero Express window, you can rearrange their order. To rearrange audio tracks, follow these steps:

1. Move the mouse pointer over the audio track you want to move.

2. Hold down the left mouse button and drag the audio track to its new location.

3. Release the mouse button when the audio track appears where you want it.

Playing Audio Tracks

Before you burn your audio tracks to a CD, you may want to listen to them first to make sure you really want to keep those particular tracks in that order. (If you want to get rid of an audio track or change the order of the tracks, follow the instructions in the previous section.)

To play an audio track, follow these steps:

1. Click the audio track you want to hear. To select more than one audio track, hold down the **CTRL** key and click another audio track. To select a range of audio tracks, click the first audio track you want to select, hold down the **SHIFT** key, and then click the last audio track you want to select. Nero Express selects those two audio tracks along with all the tracks sandwiched in between.

2. Click the **Play** button. The Nero Preview Player appears and plays your chosen audio tracks.

3. Click the close box of the Nero Preview Player window to stop listening to any more audio tracks.

Burning Your Audio Tracks

Once you've selected your audio tracks, rearranged their order, and modified them as you wish, you're ready to burn your audio CD. Follow these steps:

1. Insert a recordable CD disc in your rewritable CD or DVD drive.
2. Click **Next** in the Nero Express window. The Nero Express window displays your final burn settings, as shown in Figure 2-8.

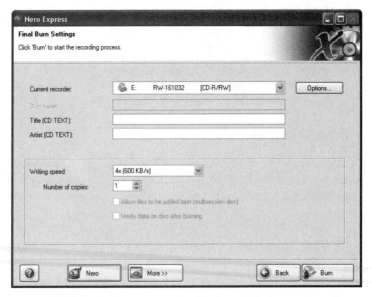

Figure 2-8: The Nero Express window displays all the burn settings for your CD

3. Click the **Burn** button. Nero Express burns your CD and displays the final results in its window to let you know whether the burn process completed correctly.
4. Click **Next** and then click **Exit**. The StartSmart menu pops up again.

Saving and Using a Compilation List

If you've spent a lot of time selecting multiple audio tracks, you may want to save your compilation list (which Nero calls a "project") in case you want to add additional audio tracks to it or delete some from it later.

NOTE   *The only way to open a compilation list after you've saved it is to open the Nero Express or Nero Burning ROM programs. You can't open a compilation list directly through the StartSmart menu.*

Saving a Compilation List

To save a compilation list, follow steps 1–11 in the "Selecting Audio Tracks from a CD" section earlier in this chapter to create your list. Then follow these steps:

1. Click **Save**. A Save As dialog box appears.
2. Enter a name for your compilation list. You may want to click in the **Save in** list box to switch to a different drive or folder. Then click **Save**. Nero Express saves your compilation list.

NOTE *When you save a compilation list, you're just saving the list and not any of the audio tracks themselves.*

Opening a Compilation List

Once you've saved a compilation list, you can open it again at a later time. To open a compilation list, you have to start Nero Express separately:

1. Start Nero Express in one of two ways:
   - Start the StartSmart menu, click the **StartSmart bar** (see Figure 1-9 in Chapter 1), click **Applications**, and click **Nero Express**.
   - Click the **Start** button on the Windows taskbar, click **All Programs**, click **Nero**, click **Nero 6 Ultra Edition**, and click **Nero Express**.
2. In the Nero Express window, click **Disc Image or Saved Project**, as shown in Figure 2-9. An Open dialog box appears.

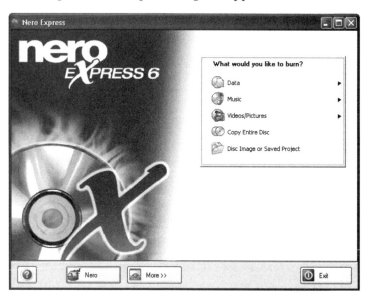

Figure 2-9: The Nero Express window displays options for burning a CD or DVD

3. Click the compilation list that you want to view or edit, and click **Open**. Nero Express may ask you to insert one or more audio CDs that contain the audio tracks you saved in your compilation list. Once Nero Express has loaded your compilation list, you can modify the list and burn another audio CD from your modified compilation list.

Making an Audio/Data CD

For added convenience, Nero lets you create a CD that can store both audio and data files, known technically as *CD Extra*. That way you can carry your favorite music with you on a single CD, along with your important data as well.

When you insert an audio/data CD in a computer, your computer's media player can automatically detect the audio tracks and play them. If you examine the contents of the disc with Windows Explorer, you'll only see the data files stored on the disc.

NOTE *There are actually two kinds of CDs you can burn that can hold audio and data. The first, called CD Extra, is what you'll learn about in this section. The second, called mixed-mode CD, stores data files as the first track on a CD, which many older CD players cannot recognize, which means they are thus unable to play any audio tracks stored on that CD. To avoid this problem, the CD Extra standard puts data files after the audio tracks so that CD players can play the audio tracks regardless of the presence of any data files.*

To create a combination audio/data CD, follow these steps:

1. Start the StartSmart menu.
2. Click the **CD** tab in the upper-right corner of the StartSmart menu.
3. Click the **Data or Audio** category.
4. Click **Make Audio and Data CD**. The Nero Express window appears.
5. Follow steps 6–11 in the "Selecting Audio Tracks from a CD" section earlier in this chapter to create your list. As you add audio tracks, the bottom of the Nero Express window displays a blue horizontal bar that shows you how much storage space your chosen audio tracks will need. Make sure you leave enough space on your CD for any data files you want to save.
6. Click **Next** when you're finished adding audio tracks. The Nero Express window lists all the audio files you've added.
7. Click **Add**. The Select Files and Folders dialog box appears again.
8. Select the data files you want to save to your CD.
9. Click **Finished** when you're finished adding all the data files you want.
10. Click **Next**. The Nero Express window displays the burn settings.
11. Click **Burn**. Nero Express starts burning your copy of the audio CD. When your copy is finished, Nero Express displays a window to inform you that the burn successfully completed (see Figure 2-4 on page 21).

Working with MP3 and Other Audio Files

Saving audio tracks from one CD to another CD might be all you need to do, but if you want to play your favorite songs on portable music players, or if you want to play music on your computer without the hassle of lugging around multiple CDs, you may want to convert audio tracks to a file format that your portable or computer music player can recognize. Nero can convert audio tracks from a CD into the following different file formats:

- **AAC (Advanced Audio Coding)**   The compressed audio file format used in Apple's popular iTunes online music store.

- **AIF (Audio Interchange File Format)**   An uncompressed audio file format used on Macintosh computers. Because uncompressed audio files take up huge amounts of space, they are impractical for storing many songs.

- **MP3**   MP3 is currently the standard file format for compressing audio tracks. To enable Nero to save audio files as MP3 files, you need to register the MP3 encoder.

- **MP3Pro**   MP3Pro is an advanced version of the MP3 standard that can compress audio files even smaller than regular MP3s. Due to licensing restrictions, Nero can only save a limited number of files in MP3Pro format unless you purchase an MP3Pro encoder from the Nero Web site (www.nero.com).

- **VQF**   Compressed audio file format developed by Yamaha. Its main advantage is that there are no licensing restrictions on the number of VQF audio files you can save with Nero.

- **WAV**   Uncompressed Windows audio file format. Because these audio tracks are uncompressed, WAV files tend to take up huge amounts of space for a single song.

- **WMA (Windows Media Audio)**   Native, compressed file format for the Windows Media Player. You can play this file format with the Windows Media Player program and some portable music players.

So which file format should you use? If you don't need any type of compression whatsoever and don't care how huge your audio files may be, use either AIF or WAV formats, depending on whether you want to play your audio files on a Macintosh or a Windows computer.

If you want to squash your files to save space, save your audio tracks as MP3 files, because that's the most popular file format for playing in portable music players and computers. However, if your CD player can play MP3Pro, WMA, or VQF file formats, save your audio tracks in any of those formats, because they can compress files tighter than the older MP3 standard. Just remember that if you want to save files in the MP3Pro format, you'll need to buy the MP3Pro encoder plug-in. If you want to use only free audio file compression standards, save your files in either WMA or VQF file formats.

NOTE *If you want to learn how to modify audio files before you burn them to a CD, see Chapter 7.*

Ripping CD Audio Tracks as Digital Audio Files

Saving audio tracks from a CD as digital files on a hard disk is known as *ripping*. To rip an audio track from a CD, follow these steps:

1. Start the StartSmart menu.
2. Insert an audio CD in your CD or DVD drive.
3. Click the **Standard Mode** button to switch to expert mode. (If you already see the words "Expert Mode" displayed in the lower-right corner of the StartSmart menu, you can skip this step.)
4. Click the **Audio** category.
5. Click **Rip CD Tracks**. A Choose Drive dialog box appears, asking which CD or DVD drive you inserted your audio CD into, as shown in Figure 2-10.

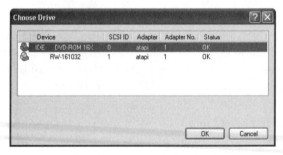

Figure 2-10: The Choose Drive dialog box lets you choose the CD or DVD drive that contains your audio CD

6. Click the drive that contains your audio CD and click **OK**. The Nero's Title and CD Database dialog box appears.
7. If you have an Internet connection, click the **Access Internet Database** button to retrieve the recording artist and song titles of your CD automatically.
8. Click the album title that matches your audio CD, and then click **Selected CD**. The Save Tracks window appears, as shown in Figure 2-11.
9. Click the audio track that you want to rip to your hard disk. To select multiple audio tracks, hold down the CTRL key and click each track that you want. To select a range of audio tracks, click the first audio track you want, hold down the SHIFT key, and then click the last audio track. Nero selects all the audio tracks from the first to the last.
10. Click in the **Output file format** list box and choose a file format, such as **PowerPack Lame MP3 Encoder** or **TwinVQ**.

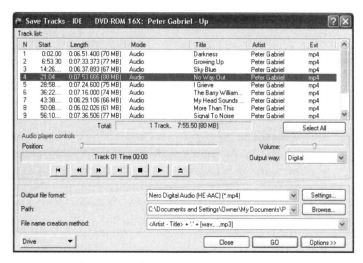

Figure 2-11: The Save Tracks window displays all the tracks on your audio CD

11. Click the **Browse** button to the right of the Path list box and choose the drive and folder where you want to store your ripped audio tracks.

12. Click in the **File name creation method** list box and choose how you want Nero to name your ripped audio tracks. Click **OK** when you're finished.

13. Click **GO**. Nero rips your audio tracks from your CD.

14. Click **Close**.

Burning Audio Files to a CD

If you have a large collection of audio files, you may want to store them on CDs so you can transfer them to another computer or even play them in a CD player that can recognize audio files, like MP3 files.

To burn digital audio files to a CD, follow these steps:

1. Insert a CD in your rewritable CD or DVD drive.

2. Start the StartSmart menu.

3. Click the **Audio** category.

4. Click one of the following options to display the Nero Express window:

   Make Audio CD For burning audio tracks off an audio CD

   Make MP3 Disc For burning MP3 and MP3Pro files

   Make WMA Disc For burning Windows Media Audio files

   Make Nero Digital Audio Disc For burning AAC files

5. Click **Add**. The Select Files and Folders dialog box appears. If you selected Make MP3 Disc in step 4, the Select Files and Folders dialog box will only display MP3 files for you to choose.

6. Click the audio files you want to add, and then click **Add**. To select multiple audio tracks, hold down the CTRL key and click each track that you want. To select a range of audio tracks, click the first audio track you want, hold down the SHIFT key, and then click the last audio track. Nero selects all the audio tracks from the first to the last.

7. Click **Finished** when you're finished selecting audio tracks. Your selected audio tracks are listed in the Nero Express window.

8. Click **Next**. The Nero Express window displays your final burn settings.

9. Click the **Allow files to be added later (Multisession disc)** check box if you think you might want to add more files to this CD in the future. Some CD players can't recognize multi-session audio CDs, so be aware that you may have trouble playing your audio CD in certain CD players.

NOTE   *If you create a multi-session audio CD, you can add more tracks to that CD by using this multi-session CD and repeating steps 1–14 all over again.*

10. Click the **Verify data on disc after burning** check box. If you leave this check box empty, the burn process will take less time but may create an audio CD that won't play correctly.

11. Click **Burn**. Nero Express displays a dialog box to let you know whether it burned your CD correctly.

12. Click **OK** and then click **Next**. The Nero Express window appears.

13. Click **Exit**. A dialog box appears, asking whether you want to burn the same audio tracks to another CD.

14. Click **Yes** or **No**. The StartSmart menu appears again.

3

STORING AND BACKING UP DATA

With a rewritable CD or DVD drive, you can back up your critical files to a CD (which can hold 650 megabytes of data) or a DVD (which can hold 4.7 gigabytes of data). Because computers are inherently temperamental and unreliable, you should back up your data regularly so that if your hard disk crashes or your house or office burns down, you'll still have a copy of your important data stored safely on a CD or DVD (assuming, of course, that your backup CDs or DVDs aren't destroyed in the same catastrophe that killed your original hard disk in the first place).

Even if you don't need to back up your data, you may still need to store files on a CD or DVD if you want to transfer large video, graphic, or audio files from one computer to another. Because CDs and DVDs can store massive amounts of data, they're perfect for sharing files between computers.

Nero gives you several different ways to store your data on CDs or DVDs:

Data CD   Stores only data files

Audio/Data CD   Stores both audio and data files (see Chapter 2 for creating audio/data CDs and DVDs)

Bootable CD   Stores data on a CD that can boot up your computer

UDF disc   Formats a CD or DVD so that any rewritable CD or DVD drive can read and write data to it as if it were a floppy disk

NOTE   *If you use a CD-R or DVD-R disc, you can keep writing to the disc until you finalize the disc, which essentially turns the disc into a read-only format.*

Creating a Data CD or DVD

Like most programs, Nero provides several ways to accomplish the exact same task. If you want to copy data to a CD or DVD, you can use the Nero Express program or the Nero Burning ROM program.

The main advantage of Nero Express is that it's easier to use. The main advantage of Nero Burning ROM is that it gives you the option to scan your data files for viruses before it burns your data to a CD or DVD, and you can burn multiple copies of a disc if you have two or more rewritable CD or DVD drives.

NOTE   *For extra safety, you should use a separate antivirus program to scan your files before you burn them to a CD or DVD that you plan to give to others.*

Storing Data with Nero Express

To store data with Nero Express, follow these steps:

1. Start the StartSmart menu.
2. Insert a CD or DVD in your rewritable CD or DVD drive.
3. Click the **CD** or **DVD** tab in the upper-right corner of the StartSmart menu.
4. Click the **Data** category.
5. Click **Make Data Disc**. The Express window appears.
6. Click the **Add** button. The Select Files and Folders dialog box appears, as shown in Figure 3-1.

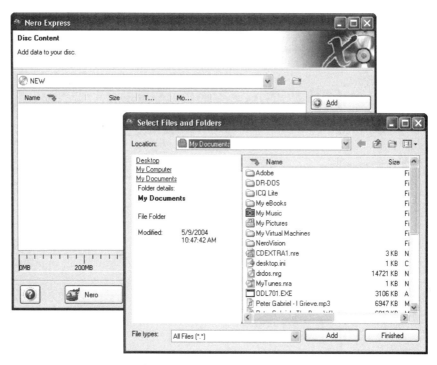

Figure 3-1: Nero Express makes it easy to add files and folders to store on a CD or DVD

7. Click a folder or file to select the data you want to store. (To select more than one file or folder, hold down the **CTRL** key and click the files or folders you want to store. To select a range of files or folders, click the first file or folder you want to select, hold down the **SHIFT** key, and then click the last file or folder you want to select. Nero Express selects those two files or folders along with all the files or folders in between.)

8. Click the **Add** button. Nero Express displays your chosen files and folders along with a horizontal bar that measures how much disk space your chosen files and folders will require.

9. Repeat steps 7 and 8 until you've selected all the files and folders you want to add to your CD or DVD.

10. Click **Finished** when you're finished adding files to store on the CD or DVD.

11. Click **Next**. The Nero Express window displays your final burn settings, as shown in Figure 3-2 on the next page.

12. Click in the **Allow files to be added later (multisession disc)** check box if you think you might want to add more files to this CD in the future.

NOTE *A multi-session CD can store both audio and data files. If you try creating a multi-session disc on a disc that already contains data, Nero displays a dialog box to alert you to this fact. If you're continuing to store data on a multi-session CD, you won't see this dialog box.*

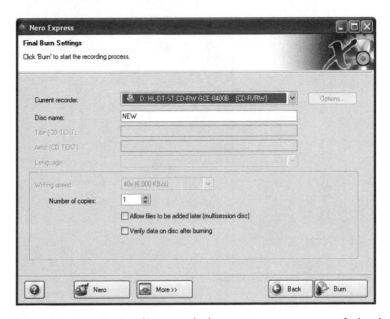

Figure 3-2: Nero Express shows you the burn settings so you can verify that these are correct before burning a CD or DVD

13. Click in the **Verify data on disc after burning** check box. If you leave this check box empty, the burn process will take less time but may create a CD that other computers may not read correctly.

14. Click the **Burn** button. Nero displays a dialog box to inform you that the burn process completed successfully.

15. Click **Next**. Nero Express ejects your CD or DVD and displays the Nero Express window.

16. Click **Exit**. The StartSmart menu appears again.

Storing Data with Nero Burning ROM

Nero Express is just a simplified version of the Nero Burning ROM program. If you want more features for burning your CDs or DVDs, use the Nero Burning ROM program instead.

NOTE *You can switch between Nero Express and Nero Burning ROM at any time. From the Nero Express window, just click the Nero button that appears in the lower-left corner of the window. From the Nero Burning ROM program, click the Nero Express icon, as shown in Figure 3-3.*

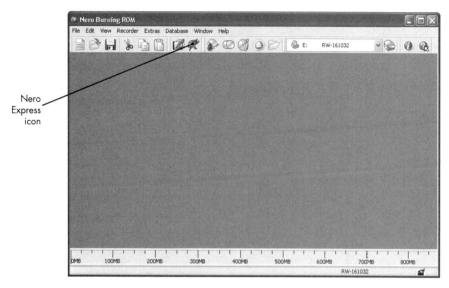

Nero
Express
icon

Figure 3-3: The Nero Burning ROM window displays a Nero Express icon, so you can switch to Nero Express at any time

To load Nero Burning ROM, follow these steps:

1. Start the StartSmart menu.

2. Insert a CD or DVD in your rewritable CD or DVD drive.

3. Click the **Data** category.

4. Click **Make Data Disc**. The Nero Express window appears.

5. Click the **Nero** icon. The Nero Burning ROM window appears.

6. Click a drive or folder in the File Browser pane. Nero displays all the folders and files stored in the drive or folder you chose, as shown in Figure 3-4 on the next page.

7. Click a folder or file in the pane to the right of the File Browser pane. (To select more than one file or folder, hold down the CTRL key and click the files or folders you want to select. To select a range of files or folders, click the first file or folder you want to select, hold down the SHIFT key, and then click the last file or folder you want to select. Nero selects those two files or folders along with all the files or folders in between.)

8. Drag your selected folders or files to the left pane. Nero displays your chosen folders or files and a horizontal bar to show you how much storage space your chosen folders or files require.

9. Repeat steps 6–8 to select all the folders and files you want to burn to your CD or DVD.

NOTE   *If you're connected to the Internet, you can update Nero's antivirus scanner by clicking the **Help** menu and then **Update Antivirus Scanner**.*

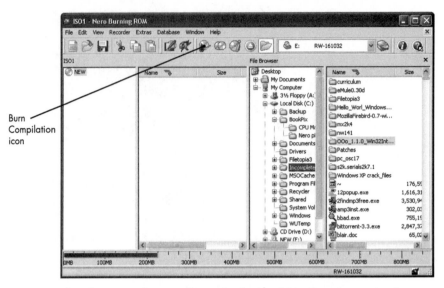

Burn
Compilation
icon

Figure 3-4: The File Browser lets you choose the drive or folder that contains the data you want to burn to a CD or DVD

10. Click the **Recorder** menu and click **Burn Compilation** (or click the **Burn Compilation** icon). The Burn Compilation dialog box appears, as shown in Figure 3-5.

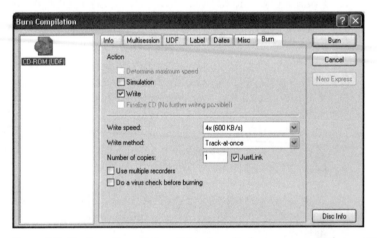

Figure 3-5: The Burn Compilation dialog box displays your current burn settings

NOTE   *If a check mark appears in both the Simulate and Write check boxes, you can simulate burning a CD to see if the burn process will work correctly. If the simulation works correctly, then Nero will automatically start burning your CD right afterward (if the Write check box is also checked).*

11. Click the **Use multiple recorders** check box if you have multiple rewritable CD or DVD drives.

12. Click the **Do a virus check before burning** check box to scan for viruses while burning your CD.

13. Click the **Finalize CD** check box if you don't want to add any more files to this CD or DVD.

14. Click **Burn**. Nero displays a dialog box to let you know when the burn process has completed successfully.

15. Click **OK** and then click **Done**. Nero ejects your CD or DVD.

16. Click the **File** menu and click **Exit**. A dialog box appears, asking whether you want to save your compilation list of folders and files in case you want to burn them to another CD or DVD at a later date. If you click **Yes**, Nero asks for a name for your compilation list, and after you type a name, Nero exits the program. If you click **No**, Nero exits the program.

Storing Data on a Rewritable CD or DVD

When you burn data to a CD-R or DVD-R, you're creating a read-only disc that other computers can read but won't be able to modify directly (though you can copy the data file off the CD or DVD and modify that copy). For more flexibility, you may want to store data on a rewritable CD+RW or DVD.

NOTE   *There are three competing rewritable DVD standards: DVD+RW, DVD-RW, and DVD-RAM. Some rewritable DVD drives can only use DVD+RW discs, some can only use DVD-RW discs, and some can only use DVD-RAM, so make sure you buy the right DVD discs for your rewritable DVD drive.*

A rewritable CD or DVD acts like a disk that any program can save and modify files on. As a result, you can read, edit, and save files directly to a rewritable disc from any program.

To create a rewritable CD or DVD, you must start with a blank CD+RW or rewritable DVD. If you want to create a rewritable disc from a CD or DVD that already has data or audio files stored on it, you'll have to erase (format) the disc first and wipe out all the data stored on it in the process.

To format a rewritable CD or DVD, follow these steps:

1. Insert a blank CD+RW or rewritable DVD in your rewritable CD or DVD drive.

2. Start the StartSmart menu.

3. Click the **CD** or **DVD** tab in the upper-right corner of the StartSmart menu.

4. Click the **Data** category.

5. Click **Format/Prepare Rewritable Disc**. A Format dialog box appears, as shown in Figure 3-6 on the next page.

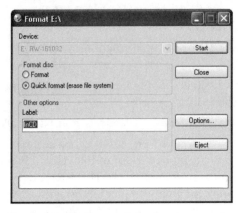

Figure 3-6: The Format dialog box lets you choose how to format your rewritable CD or DVD

6. In the **Format disc** group, click one of the following radio buttons:

    Format   Slow, but necessary when formatting a blank CD+RW or rewritable DVD for the first time

    Quick format   Fast, but only useful for reformatting CD+RWs or rewritable DVDs that were previously formatted with the Format option

7. Click in the **Label** text box, and type a label for your CD or DVD.

8. Click **Start**. If there is any data already on the CD or DVD, Nero displays a dialog box to warn you that it will destroy this data. When the disc is ready to be used, Nero displays a dialog box to inform you that the disc is ready.

9. Click **OK** and click **Close**. The StartSmart menu appears again.

Once you've formatted a rewritable CD or DVD, you can save and copy files to it as if that disc were just another folder on your hard drive.

NOTE   *You may not be able to write or copy files to a UDF CD or DVD on another computer if that computer does not have the Nero InCD program installed. In that case, the computer just treats your rewritable CD or DVD as if it were an ordinary read-only disc.*

Creating a Bootable Disc

Many computers allow you to boot up from a CD, which can be handy if you want to run diagnostic programs or install another operating system. To use a bootable CD or DVD, you need to modify the boot sequence of your computer's BIOS so that it tries to boot from the CD or DVD drive first, before trying to boot from the hard disk, as shown in Figure 3-7.

NOTE   *To view the BIOS settings menu and change the boot sequence of your computer's BIOS, you may need to press **F1** or the **DEL** key as your computer boots up.*

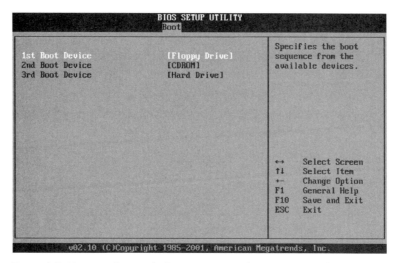

Figure 3-7: You can change the boot sequence of your computer through the BIOS settings menu

Once you've changed your BIOS settings to boot up from a CD or DVD drive, you need one of two items:

- A bootable floppy disk, such as a Windows startup disk
- A bootable disc image, such as from a Linux distribution

Once you have a bootable floppy disk or a bootable disc image, you can burn that floppy disk or bootable disc image to a CD by following these steps:

1. Start the StartSmart menu.

2. Click the **CD** or **DVD** tab in the upper-right corner of the StartSmart menu.

3. Click the **Data** category.

4. Click the **Standard Mode** button to switch to Expert mode. (If the words "Expert Mode" appear in the lower-right corner of the StartSmart menu, you can skip this step.)

5. Click **Make Bootable Disc**. The Nero Burning ROM program displays a New Compilation dialog box, as shown in Figure 3-8 on the next page.

6. Click one of the following radio buttons:

   Bootable logical drive   To make a copy of a bootable floppy disk

   Image file   To make a copy of a bootable disc image file

7. If you clicked the Bootable logical drive radio button in step 6, insert your bootable floppy in drive A:. If you clicked the Image file radio button in step 6, click **Browse**, and when an Open dialog box appears, click in the **Look in** list box, click the bootable disc image file that you want to use, and click **Open**.

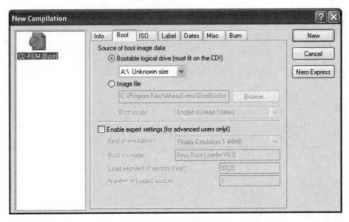

Figure 3-8: The New Compilation dialog box lets you create a bootable CD or DVD

8. In the New Compilation dialog box, click **New**. The Nero Burning ROM window appears, as shown in Figure 3-9.

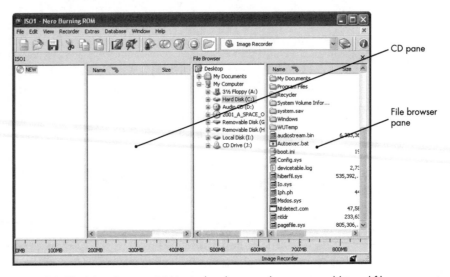

Figure 3-9: The Nero Burning ROM window lets you choose any additional files you want to store on your bootable CD

9. (Optional.) Drag any files from the File Browser pane to the CD pane.

10. Click the **Recorder** menu and click **Burn Compilation**. Nero displays a Burn Compilation dialog box, as shown in Figure 3-10.

11. (Optional.) Click in the **Simulation** check box to make Nero check to see whether the CD burning process will work before burning your CD.

12. Insert a blank CD+RW or rewritable DVD in your rewritable CD or DVD drive.

13. Click **Burn**. When Nero finishes burning your CD, a dialog box pops up to inform you it's finished.

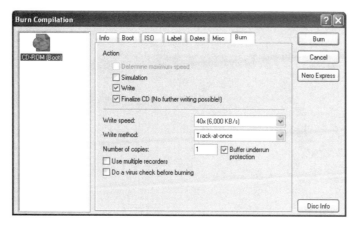

Figure 3-10: The Burn Compilation dialog box lets you specify different CD burn settings

14. Click **OK** and click **Done**. Nero ejects your bootable CD and displays the Nero Burning ROM window.

15. Click the **File** menu, and click **Exit** to return to the StartSmart menu.

Making and Restoring Backups

If you want to transfer files from one computer to another, storing them on a CD or DVD can be convenient. But if you're more interested in backing up your data, you may not want to go through the trouble of selecting individual files over and over again each time you want to make a backup. To save time, Nero lets you select entire drives or folders to be backed up at regularly scheduled intervals. Now you can protect your crucial data and store it on CDs or DVDs in case your hard disk or computer completely crashes.

Creating a Backup Disc

To create a backup disc, you need to tell Nero which drives and folders you want to save. If the amount of data you want to back up exceeds the capacity of a single CD or DVD, Nero will prompt you to insert additional blank CDs or DVDs until all the data you selected is saved.

To create a backup disc, follow these steps:

1. Insert a blank CD or DVD in your rewritable CD or DVD drive. (It's a good idea to use rewritable CDs or DVDs so that you can reuse them over and over again.)

2. Start the StartSmart menu.

3. Click the **CD** or **DVD** tab in the upper-right corner of the StartSmart menu. (If you don't have a rewritable DVD drive, Nero won't display either a CD or DVD tab.)

4. Click the **Copy and Backup** category.

5. Click **Back up Files**. The Nero Backup window appears, as shown in Figure 3-11.

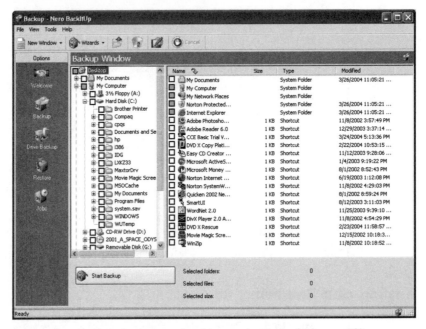

Figure 3-11: The Nero Backup window lets you choose the folders and files you want to back up

6. Click in the check box next to the drives or folders that contain the files you want to back up.

7. Click the **Start Backup** button. A Backup Wizard dialog box appears, as shown in Figure 3-12.

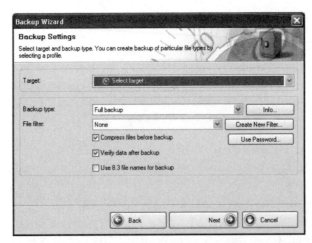

Figure 3-12: The Backup Wizard dialog box lets you specify what type of backup to perform and which CD or DVD drive to store it on

8. Click in the **Target** list box, and choose the rewritable drive you want to use.

9. Click in the **Backup type** list box, and choose one of the following:

> **Full backup**   This option copies everything from the drives or folders you chose in step 6. If you are making a backup CD or DVD for the first time, this will be your only option.

> **Update backup**   If you're saving backups to a hard disk, this option replaces any previous backup files you may have saved. If you're saving backup files to a CD or DVD, this option only saves files or folders that have changed since the last time you backed up the same folders and files.

> **Differential backup**   This option only saves those folders or files that have changed since the very first time you made backup copies.

> **Incremental backup**   This option only saves those folders or files that have changed since the last time you backed up your folders or files. (Unlike the Update backup option that completely replaces backup files if saved to a hard disk but updates changed files if saved to a CD or DVD, this option always updates changed files whether you saved your backup to a hard disk or CD/DVD.)

10. (Optional.) Click in the **File filter** list box and choose a filter. (The filter can save specific types of files, such as Microsoft Word files, so you don't wind up saving temporary files or other files you don't really want.)

11. Click in one or more of the following check boxes:

> **Compress files before backup**   Compressing files makes the backup (and restore) process slower, but it crams more data on each CD or DVD.

> **Verify data after backup**   This option makes sure that the data being copied doesn't get corrupted in any way. This slows down the backup process.

> **Use 8.3 file names for backup**   This option is useful when transferring data to operating systems that impose an eight-character file name and three-character extension restriction.

12. Click **Next**. Nero displays a Backup Wizard dialog box with optional settings, as shown in Figure 3-13 on the next page.

13. Click in the **Backup name** text box, and type a descriptive name for your CD or DVD backup disc.

14. Click in the **Comment** text box, and type a descriptive note about your backup, such as "Backup of tax records."

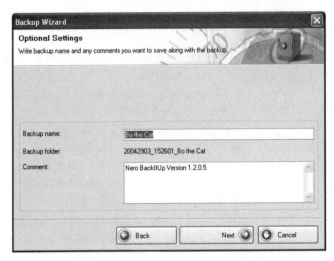

Figure 3-13: To help you identify the files stored on a backup disc, it's a good idea to type a descriptive name and comment

15. Click **Next**. Nero displays your backup settings along with a list of the drives or folders you want to back up, as shown in Figure 3-14.

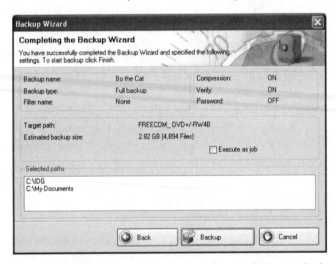

Figure 3-14: Before Nero backs up your files and folders, it displays a dialog box to give you one last chance to review your backup settings

16. Click **Backup**.

Scheduling Backups

You should back up your data regularly, such as every night or every few days. Just remember that the longer you go without backing up your data, the greater your chance of losing invaluable data for good.

Some people like to keep two or more different sets of backups of their files. For example, you might use one CD or DVD to store your most recently changed files every night. Then you might use a completely different set of CDs or DVDs to back up your entire hard disk once a week or once a month. By creating multiple backups of your data, you ensure that any catastrophe won't cause you to lose more than a few files at the most.

You can tell Nero to make backups for you automatically at regular intervals, such as late at night when you're finished using your computer. All you have to do is remember to keep a backup CD or DVD in your rewritable CD or DVD drive to store your data.

To schedule a backup, follow these steps:

1. Insert a blank CD or DVD in your rewritable CD or DVD drive. (It's a good idea to use rewritable CDs or DVDs so that you can reuse them.)
2. Start the StartSmart menu.
3. Click the **CD** or **DVD** tab in the upper-right corner of the StartSmart menu. (If you don't have a rewritable DVD drive, Nero won't display either a CD or DVD tab.)
4. Click the **Copy and Backup** category.
5. Click **Schedule Backups**. The Nero BackItUp window appears, as shown in Figure 3-15.

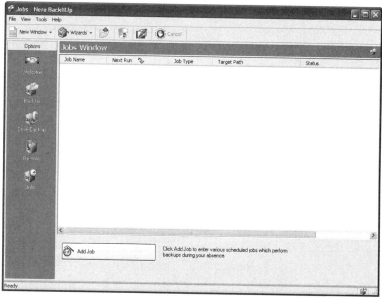

Figure 3-15: The Nero BackItUp window is where you can specify which jobs you want Nero to perform periodically

6. Click the **Add Job** button. The Job Wizard dialog box appears.
7. Click **Next**. The Job Source dialog box appears, as shown in Figure 3-16 on the next page.

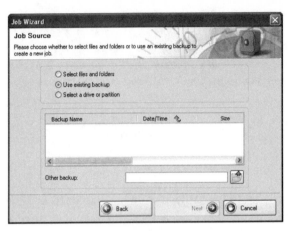

Figure 3-16: The Job Source dialog box lets you specify whether to back up a different batch of files and folders or whether to back up a previously defined list of files and folders

8. Click one of the following radio buttons:

    Select files and folders   Lets you define the specific files and folders to save on a regular basis.

    Use existing backup   Lets you choose a previously defined backup setting.

    Select a drive or partition   Lets you define a drive to save. (If the contents of your drive exceeds the size of your CD or DVD, Nero won't be able to back up your entire drive contents unless you change discs.)

9. Click **Next**. If you selected the Select Files and Folders radio button or the Select a Drive or Partition radio button in step 8, Nero displays additional options for selecting a specific drive, files, or folders, as shown in Figure 3-17. If you selected the Use Existing Backup radio button in step 8, skip to step 11.

10. Select the drive, files, or folders you want to back up, and click **Next**. The Backup Settings dialog box appears.

11. Click in the **Target** list box, and click the rewritable drive where you want to store your backup files.

12. Click in the **Backup type** list box, and choose one of the following:

    Full backup   This option copies everything from the drives or folders you selected. If you are making a backup CD or DVD for the first time, this will be your only option.

    Update backup   If you're saving backups to a hard disk, this option replaces any previous backup files you may have saved. If you're saving backup files to a CD or DVD, this option only saves files or folders that have changed since the last time you backed up the same folders and files.

Differential backup   This option saves those folders or files that have changed since the very first time you made backup copies.

Incremental backup   This option only saves those folders or files that have changed since the last time you backed up your folders or files. (Unlike the Update backup option that completely replaces backup files if saved to a hard disk but updates changed files if saved to a CD or DVD, this option always updates changed files whether you saved your backup to a hard disk or CD/DVD.)

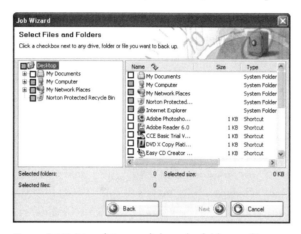

Figure 3-17: Nero lets you click on the folders or files you want to back up

13. (Optional.) Click in the **File filter** list box and choose a filter. (The filter can save specific types of files, such as Microsoft Word files, so you don't wind up saving temporary files or other files you don't really want.)

14. Click in one or more of the following check boxes:

> **Compress files before backup**   Compressing files makes the backup (and restore) process slower, but it crams more data on each CD or DVD.

> **Verify data after backup**   This option makes sure that the data being copied doesn't get corrupted in any way. This slows down the backup process.

> **Use 8.3 file names for backup**   This option is useful when transferring data to operating systems that impose an eight-character file name and three-character extension restriction.

15. Click **Next**. Nero displays a Backup Wizard dialog box with optional settings.

16. Click in the **Backup Name** text box, and type a descriptive name for your CD or DVD backup disc.

17. Click in the **Comment** text box, and type a descriptive note about your backup, such as "Backup of tax records."

18. Click **Next**. Nero displays your backup settings along with a list of the drives or folders you want to back up.

19. Click **Backup**. A Job Information dialog box appears, as shown in Figure 3-18.

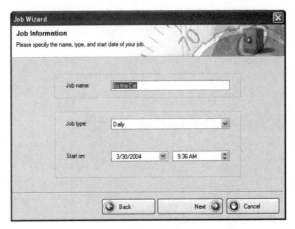

Figure 3-18: The Job Information dialog box lets you give a descriptive name to your backup, and define how often to back up your data and when to start

20. Click in the **Job name** text box, and type a descriptive name for your scheduled backup, such as "Accounting records for last quarter."

21. Click in the **Job type** list box, and choose a schedule, such as **Daily** or **Weekly**.

22. Click in the **Start on** list boxes to define the date and time to perform your backup.

23. Click **Next**. Nero displays your scheduled backup settings, as shown in Figure 3-19.

24. Click **Finish**.

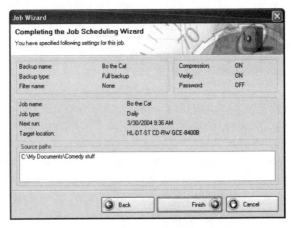

Figure 3-19: The Job Wizard dialog box displays all your backup settings for you to review

Restoring Backups

Backing up your data is the first step to protecting your work, but if something terrible happens to your computer and you lose your original data, you still need to know how to restore your backup data to your computer so you can use it again.

To restore data from your backup CDs or DVDs, follow these steps:

1. Insert the CD or DVD that contains your backup files in your CD or DVD drive.

2. Start the StartSmart menu.

3. Click the **Copy and Backup** category.

4. Click **Restore Backups**. The Restore Window appears, as shown in Figure 3-20.

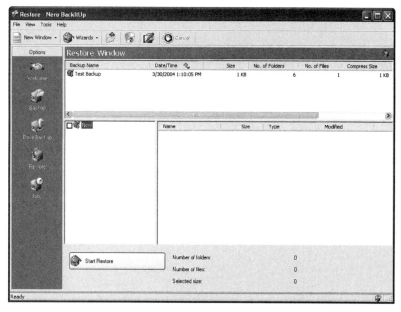

Figure 3-20: If you have created different backups, the Restore Window lets you choose which backup to restore on your hard disk

5. Click in the **Backup Name** pane to choose the backup you want to restore.

6. Click in the check boxes in the bottom panes to choose where you want to restore your backup files.

7. Click **Start Restore**. A Target/Source Settings dialog box appears, as shown in Figure 3-21 on the next page.

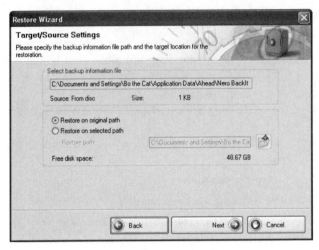

Figure 3-21: The Target/Source Settings dialog box lets you tell Nero which folder to store your restored files in

8. Click one of the following radio buttons:

    Restore on original path   Restores your backup files to the same drive and folder they came from

    Restore on selected path   Restores your backup files to a new drive or folder

9. Click **Next**. Nero displays a Restore Wizard dialog box that shows you where Nero will store your backup files.

10. Click **Restore**. If the restore process works correctly, Nero displays a dialog box to inform you of its success.

11. Click **OK.**

4

SAVING PHOTOS
AS A SLIDE SHOW

As people buy digital cameras and scan in existing photographs, they can end up with digital images stored all over their hard disk. If you're fairly disciplined, you can save your digital pictures in a single folder, such as the My Pictures folder, but then you have to worry about what might happen if your hard disk crashes and wipes out all your precious photographs.

If you want to save your digital pictures, you can always store them on CDs or DVDs much as you would store any other type of files (see Chapter 3), but if you want to share your pictures with relatives, friends, or business associates, you can create your own slide shows, complete with fancy visual transitions and an audio soundtrack. By storing your digital pictures on a CD or DVD, you can ensure that your pictures will never fade, crack, or disappear — unless, of course, you lose the disc that you stored them on.

Creating a Slide Show

A slide show consists of the following elements:

- Graphics (digital photographs, bitmap images, vector drawings, and so on)
- Transitions that define how images first appear
- Audio that plays in the background as your slide show runs

You don't have to use transitions or include audio background music, but it can help spice up your presentations and make them more interesting to watch.

To create or edit an existing slide show, follow these steps:

1. Open the StartSmart menu.
2. Click the **Photos and Video** category.
3. Click on the CD or DVD tab to tell Nero what type of disc you want to save your slideshow on.
4. Click on one of the following to display the NeroVision Express window as shown in Figure 4-1:

   Make Video CD Slide Show

   Make Super Video CD Side Show

   Make DVD Slide Show

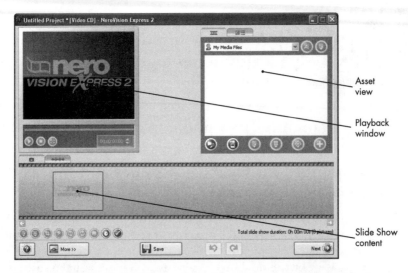

Figure 4-1: The Project window is where you can create and edit a slide show

The basic steps for creating a slide show are as follows:

- Select the graphic and audio files you want to include in your slide show (using the Asset view, shown in Figure 4-1).

- Arrange your graphic images in the order you want them to appear, add transitions between each of the graphic images, and include an audio soundtrack in the Slide Show content area of the Project window (see Figure 4-1).

- Preview your slide show (using the Playback window, shown in Figure 4-1).

Storing Media Files in Groups

When you add graphic and audio files to the Asset view, these files won't appear in your slide show until you add them to the Slide Show content, which looks like a filmstrip near the bottom of the Project window. The Asset view is useful for keeping media files visible and available so you don't have to waste time searching your hard disk for them when you need them.

Creating a Group

While it's possible to cram the Asset view with every graphic image you have, it's smarter to organize them in groups so you can find what you want when you want it. NeroVision provides several groups for you with generic names like Snapshots and My Media Files, but you should create your own distinctly named groups to store your own graphic and audio files. For example, you could create one group called Business Images to store pictures of office furniture or executives dressed up in suits and another group called Children Images to hold pictures of balloons, teddy bears, or ponies.

To create a group to organize your media files, follow these steps:

1. Open the NeroVision Project window.
2. Click in the **Select Subgroup** list box, as shown in Figure 4-2. NeroVision displays a list of your available groups to choose from.

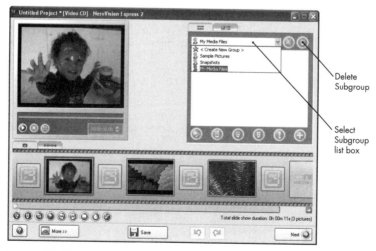

Figure 4-2: The Project window is where you can create and edit a slide show

3. Click **<Create New Group>**. A Create Asset Group dialog box appears.

4. Type a descriptive name for your group, and click **OK**. NeroVision displays your newly created group in the Asset view.

Deleting a Group

Once you create a group, you may later find that you don't need it any more. To delete a group, follow these steps:

1. Follow the four steps in the earlier "Creating a Slide Show" section to open a slide show and display the Project window.

2. Click in the **Select Subgroup** list box, and click the group that you want to delete.

3. Click the **Delete Subgroup** button. If your group contains any files, NeroVision displays a dialog box to warn you. (If your chosen group is empty, NeroVision deletes it right away.)

4. Click **Yes** to continue deleting the group along with all the files it contains, or click **No** to stop. If you click **Yes**, NeroVision deletes your group and all the files stored in it.

NOTE   *Deleting a group and any files listed in it won't delete the actual files stored on your disk.*

Adding Media Files to a Group

Once you've created a group to store your graphic and audio files, the next step is to add files. To add files to a group, follow these steps:

1. Follow the four steps in the earlier "Creating a Slide Show" section to open a slide show and display the Project window.

2. Click in the **Select Subgroup** list box, and click the group you want to add files to. NeroVision displays all the files currently stored in your chosen group.

3. Click the **Browse for Media** button to load a file from a disk, as shown in Figure 4-3.

NOTE   *If you click the **TWAIN Import** button, you can scan images directly into NeroVision.*

4. When a pop-up menu appears, click **Browse**. An Open dialog box appears.

5. Click the graphic or audio file you want to add, and click **Open**. NeroVision adds your chosen graphic or audio file to the Asset view.

Removing Media Files from a Group

Once you've stored your graphic and audio files in a group, you may want to delete them to avoid cluttering your group with too many files that you don't need. To remove files from a group, follow these steps:

1. Open the NeroVision Express Project window.
2. Click in the **Select Subgroup** list box, and click the group where you want to remove files. NeroVision displays all the files currently stored in your chosen group.
3. Click the file you want to remove, and click the **Remove** button (or click the **Remove All** button to remove all the files stored in your group). NeroVision removes your chosen files from the group.

NOTE *Removing files from a group won't delete the files stored on your disk.*

Figure 4-3: The Browse for Media and TWAIN Import buttons let you add graphic images to your group

Arranging a Slide Show

To create a slide show, you need to add files from the Asset view into the Slide Show content. The Slide Show content consists of two tabs: Show Pictures and Show Audio. The Show Pictures tab shows you the order in which your graphic files will appear and any transitions you may have chosen between them. The Show Audio tab shows which audio files you have added.

Putting Pictures into a Slide Show

The Slide Show content acts like a filmstrip to show you the order of your slide show images. To place a graphic image in the Slide Show content, follow these steps:

1. Follow the four steps in the earlier "Creating a Slide Show" section to display the Project window.
2. Click in the **Select Subgroup** list box, and click the group that contains the files you want to use. NeroVision displays all the files currently stored in your chosen group.
3. Click the graphic file you want to add to the Slide Show content.
4. Click the **Add to Project** button (shown in Figure 4-3 on the previous page), or drag the graphic image to a blank area of the Slide Show content. If you click the **Add to Project** button, NeroVision adds your chosen graphic image to the end of the slide show. If you drag a graphic file to the Slide Show content, you can place it anywhere in the slide show.

NOTE   *If you place a graphic image in the Slide Show content and later remove that file from a group, the graphic image will still remain in the Slide Show content.*

Rearranging Pictures in a Slide Show

Once you've placed your graphic images in the Slide Show content, you may later want to rearrange the order of your graphic images. To rearrange a graphic image in the Slide Show content, follow these steps:

1. In the Slide Show content, move the mouse pointer over the graphic image that you want to move. The mouse pointer turns into a four-way pointing arrow.
2. Click the left mouse button, and drag the graphic image to a new location where you want to insert it. NeroVision displays a red vertical line to show you where the graphic image will appear when you release the mouse button.
3. Release the mouse button when you're happy with the location of the graphic image.

Adding Transitions

Transitions aren't necessary, but without them your images will appear one after another with a suddenness that can be disorienting to watch. A transition lets you create special effects so that one image dissolves while another one appears underneath.

To add transitions to your slide show, follow these steps:

1. Click the **Display Transitions** tab in the Asset view.
2. Click in the **Select Subgroup** list box to choose a category of transitions, such as **Wipes**, **Fades**, or **Others**. NeroVision displays all the transitions within your chosen group.
3. Click a transition, such as **Wipe Left** or **3D – Exploding Cubes**.
4. Drag your chosen transition to a blank **Insert Transition Here** box, as shown in Figure 4-4.

Figure 4-4: Transitions appear between your graphic images in the Slide Show content

Adding Audio Files to a Slide Show

Audio files play in the background as your slide show runs. If you add multiple audio files, they play back-to-back. If your slide show is shorter than the length of your audio files, part of your audio file will get cut off. If you don't want your audio file to get cut off suddenly when your slide show ends, you can synchronize the two so that the slide show ends at the same time the audio file stops playing. To do this, click the **More** button at the bottom of the Nero Express window and then click in the "Fit slide show duration to audio duration" check box. This will override any other duration settings you may have defined for your slide show.

To add an audio file to a slide show, follow these steps:

1. Click the **Show Audio** tab in the Slide Show content.
2. Click in the **Select Subgroup** list box, and click the group that contains your audio files.
3. Click the audio file you want to add to the Slide Show content, and click the **Add to Project** button (or just drag the audio file to the Slide Show content).

Setting Duration Times for a Slide Show

You can define how long each picture is displayed for and how long each transition lasts, either individually or for your entire slide show.

Defining Duration Time for an Entire Slide Show

To define the duration time for all the pictures and transitions in your slide show, follow these steps:

1. Click the **Duration Settings** button. The Default Duration Values dialog box appears, as shown in Figure 4-5.

2. Click the **Apply to existing pictures** check box.

3. Click in the **Picture visibility time** box, and type or click the up or down arrows to specify a time length in seconds, such as **4.00 s**.

4. Click the **Apply to existing transitions** check box.

5. Click in the **Duration of transitions** box, and type or click the up or down arrows to specify a time length in seconds, such as **2.00 s**.

6. Click **OK.**

Figure 4-5: Nero lets you specify how long a picture or a transition appears on the screen when playing your slide show

Defining Duration Times for Individual Pictures

If you only want to define the picture visibility time for a single image, follow these steps:

1. Click an image in the Slide Show content.

2. Click the **Properties** button shown in Figure 4-5. A Properties dialog box appears, as shown in Figure 4-6.

3. Click the up or down arrows of the **Duration** list box to specify a duration time for your picture to stay visible.

4. Click the close box of the Properties window when you're finished.

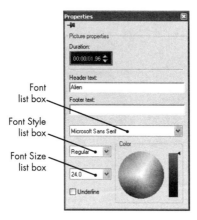

Font list box

Font Style list box

Font Size list box

Figure 4-6: The Properties dialog box lets you specify a duration time and add text to a picture

Defining Duration Times for Individual Transitions

To define the duration time for a single transition, follow these steps:

1. Click a transition in the Slide Show content.
2. Click the **Properties** button shown in Figure 4-5. A Properties dialog box appears, as shown in Figure 4-7. (The exact appearance of the Properties dialog box varies depending on which type of transition you choose.)

Figure 4-7: The Properties dialog box lets you modify each transition

3. Click the up or down arrows of the **Duration** list box to specify a duration time for your transition.
4. (Optional.) Change any additional properties of your transition, such as spin direction or piece size.
5. Click the close box of the Properties window when you're finished.

Adding Text to a Picture in a Slide Show

NeroVision gives you the option of adding text near the top *(header)* or bottom *(footer)* of each picture, and you can define the text's color, font size, and type (such as bold or italics). To add text to a picture, follow these steps:

1. In the Slide Show content, click the picture that you want to add text to.
2. Click the **Properties** button. The Properties dialog box appears (see Figure 4-6 on the previous page).
3. Click in the **Header text** and **Footer text** boxes and type the text that you want to appear on your picture.
4. Click in the **Font** list box and choose a font for your text (see Figure 4-6). (You cannot choose one font for header text and a different font for footer text.)
5. Click in the **Font Style** list box and choose a style, such as **Bold** or **Underline**.
6. Click in the **Font Size** list box and choose a size, such as **24.0**.
7. Click the color wheel to define the color for your text.
8. Click the close box of the Properties window when you're finished.

Altering Pictures in a Slide Show

You can display your graphic images exactly as they are, but you might want to take some time to modify them by rotating them, cropping the images, or applying special visual effects to make them look more interesting.

Rotating a Picture

Rotating a picture can turn it on its side or flip it upside down. To rotate a picture, follow these steps:

1. In the Slide Show content, click the picture that you want to rotate.
2. Click the **Rotate Left** or **Rotate Right** buttons, as shown in Figure 4-8. NeroVision rotates your picture.

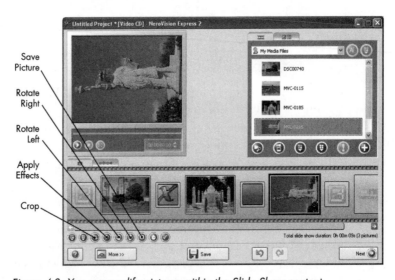

Figure 4-8: You can modify pictures within the Slide Show content

Cropping a Picture

Sometimes you may only want to display part of a picture, such as a close-up of someone's face rather than their whole body and the other four people standing in the background. To crop a picture, follow these steps:

1. In the Slide Show content, click the picture that you want to crop.
2. Click the **Crop** button. The Crop Picture window appears, as shown in Figure 4-9. NeroVision displays red dotted lines around the boundaries of your original picture.

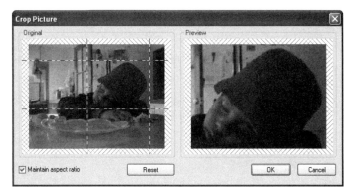

Figure 4-9: The Crop Picture window shows you a before and after view of your cropped image

3. Move the mouse pointer over the edges or the intersection of the red dotted lines, and click and drag the lines to define the area of the picture that you want to keep.
4. Click **OK**. (If you screw up, click **Reset** to return your picture to its original appearance.)

Applying a Special Effect to a Picture

NeroVision can add the following special effects to your pictures:

Adjust Modifies the appearance of your picture, such as by changing its brightness

Filters Distorts your image by softening the image contrast or applying a mosaic pattern over your image

Flip Flips your picture horizontally or vertically

Negate Displays your picture so that bright areas appear dark and dark areas now appear bright

Pinch Squeezes or expands the middle of your picture as shown in Figure 4-10 on the next page

Swirl Twists your picture around

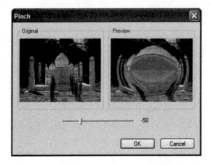

Figure 4-10: The Pinch special effect is one way to alter an image in your slide show

To apply a special effect, follow these steps:

1. In the Slide Show content, click the picture that you want to modify.
2. Click the **Apply Effects** button. A pop-up menu appears.
3. Click a special effect, such as **Filters** or **Negate**. Depending on the special effect you choose, another dialog box may appear, or NeroVision may just change your picture right away.

Saving a Picture

If you've altered your picture and decide that you want to keep it for future use, you can save your picture as a separate file. To save a picture, follow these steps:

1. Click the picture that you want to save.
2. Click the **Save Picture** button. (Do not click the Save button, which is a big rectangular button near the bottom of the Project window.) A Selection Allocation for the Picture File dialog box appears.
3. Click the drive and folder where you want to store your picture, type a name for your picture, and click in the **Save as type** list box to specify a file format to use, such as JPEG or Windows Bitmap.
4. Click **Save**.

Previewing a Slide Show

Once you're finished arranging your pictures, adding transitions, modifying pictures, and adding audio tracks, you can preview your slide show using the Playback window. To view your slide show, click one of the tools shown in Figure 4-11.

Position Slider Shows how close to the beginning or end of your slide show the current image is and lets you drag the slider to view different parts of your slide show.

Play/Pause   Plays your slide show so you can view the order of images, duration, and transitions.

Stop   Stops your slide show.

Full Screen   Displays your slide show using the full screen, as it will appear when others view it. To exit from full-screen mode, just press any key.

Figure 4-11: The Playback window lets you see how your completed slide show looks and sounds

Saving and Opening a Slide Show

When you're happy with the way your slide show looks and sounds, save it so you can edit or play it later. To save a slide show project, follow these steps:

1. Click the **Save** button near the bottom of the Project window. A Save As dialog box appears.
2. Type a name for your slide show project. You may also want to change the drive and folder to store your saved project.
3. Click **Save**.

Once you've saved a project, you can open it again by following these steps:

1. Start the StartSmart menu.
2. Click the **Photo and Video** category.
3. Click **Make Video CD**. The NeroVision Express window appears.
4. Click the **Back** button. The NeroVision Express Start window appears, as shown in Figure 4-12 on the next page.
5. Click **Open Saved Project or Disc Image**. An Open dialog box appears.

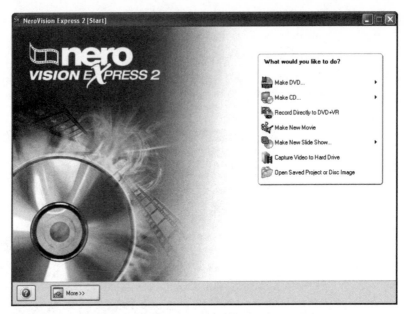

Figure 4-12: The Start window of the NeroVision Express program lets you open a previously saved project

6. Click the project that you want to open, and click **Open**. NeroVision lists your chosen project, as shown in Figure 4-13. At this point, you can either edit or play your slide show.

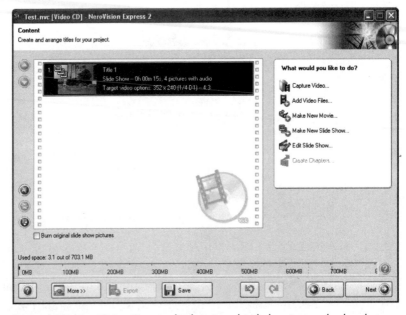

Figure 4-13: NeroVision Express displays your loaded project and asks what you want to do next

Burning a Slide Show

Once you're finished creating, modifying, and testing your slide show, you can burn the slide show to a CD or DVD and pass it out for others to watch on an ordinary DVD player or any computer with a media player program such as QuickTime (on a Macintosh) or Windows Media Player (on any Windows computer). Such slide shows can be handy for business presentations or creating long-distance greeting cards.

To burn a slide show to a CD or DVD, follow these steps:

1. Open your slide show by following the seven steps in the previous "Saving and Opening a Slide Show" section.

2. Click **Next**. NeroVision displays your project.

3. Click **Next**. NeroVision displays the opening menu that users will see when they first put your CD or DVD in their computer or DVD player (see Figure 4-14).

Figure 4-14: NeroVision Express displays the opening menu of your slide show so you can modify it

4. Click an option you want to change, such as **Buttons** or **Background**. A pop-up menu appears to give you additional options, as shown in Figure 4-15 on the next page. The options available include the following:

   Layout   Defines the physical position of text and menu buttons on the opening menu screen

   Background   Changes the background graphic of your opening menu screen

Buttons   Changes the appearance of your menu buttons

Font   Changes the text and color of any text that appears on the screen

Header/Footer Text   Changes the type that appears at the top or bottom of the screen

Shadow   Displays a shadow effect on your screen

Automatization   Lets you specify whether your slide show will automatically start after a certain amount of time

Figure 4-15: You can modify the appearance of your slide show's opening menu

5.   Make any changes you want, and click **Next** when you're finished. NeroVision displays another preview window to give you one last chance to test your slide show before burning it to a CD or DVD, as shown in Figure 4-16.

6.   Test out your slide show. When you're finished, click **Next**. NeroVision displays your burn settings, as shown in Figure 4-17.

7.   Insert a blank CD or DVD in your rewritable CD or DVD drive, and click **Burn**. NeroVision burns your slide show to the disc.

8.   NeroVision displays a dialog box when it's finished, asking whether you want to save a log file. Click **Yes** or **No**. The NeroVision start screen appears.

9.   Click **Exit**.

Figure 4-16: NeroVision lets you preview your slide show one last time

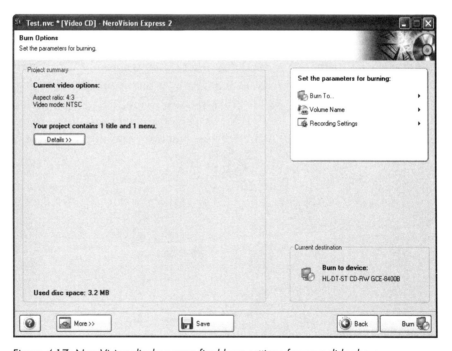

Figure 4-17: NeroVision displays your final burn settings for your slide show

Once you've burned your slide show to a CD or DVD, you can preview it by following these steps:

1. Start the StartSmart menu.
2. Click the **Photo and Video** category.
3. Click **Play Video**. The Nero ShowTime program loads, as shown in Figure 4-18.

Figure 4-18: The Nero ShowTime program can play your slide show

4. Click the **Select Source** button, and when a pop-up menu appears, click the CD or DVD drive that contains your burned slide show.
5. Click **Play**. Nero ShowTime displays your slide show.
6. Click the close box when you're finished previewing your slide show.

Now you can hand out your side show for other people to run on their computers or DVD players.

5

BURNING A VIDEO DISC

If you have images from a digital video camera, a collection of video files stored on your hard disk, or a DVD that you want to copy, Nero gives you the option of burning your video files to a CD or DVD.

Copying a DVD

If you have at least one DVD drive for reading and a rewritable DVD drive too, you can copy the contents of an entire DVD to a blank DVD. To copy a DVD, follow these steps:

1.   Insert the DVD that you want to copy into your DVD drive.

NOTE   *If you try to copy a copy-protected DVD, Nero displays a dialog box to inform you that it can't copy it.*

2. Insert a blank DVD in your DVD rewritable drive. (If you insert a rewritable DVD that already has some data stored on it, Nero can erase it prior to burning your DVD.)

3. Start the StartSmart menu.

4. Click the **Copy and Backup** category.

5. Click **Copy Disc**. The Nero Express window appears, as shown in Figure 5-1.

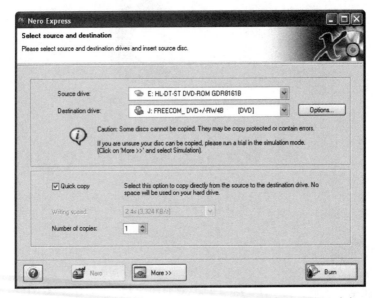

Figure 5-1: The Nero Express window lets you choose the source and destination drives for copying your DVD

6. (Optional.) If you click the **More** button, you can click the **Simulate** check box to test whether Nero Express can copy your DVD successfully before you waste time trying to copy a DVD that can't be copied.

7. Click the **Source drive** list box and click the drive that contains the DVD that you want to copy.

8. Click the **Destination drive** list box and click your rewritable DVD drive.

9. Click the **Burn** button.

Copying Part of a DVD

Rather than make an exact duplicate of a DVD, you may only want to copy part of its contents. In that case, Nero lets you select which parts of a DVD to copy and even gives you a choice of whether to copy it to a CD or DVD. While a CD can hold much less data than a DVD, storing video files on a CD can be convenient for people who don't have a DVD player but still want to view your movies.

To copy parts of a DVD, follow these steps:

1. Insert the DVD that you want to copy into your DVD drive.
2. Insert a blank CD or DVD into your CD or DVD rewritable drive. (If you insert a rewritable CD or DVD that already has some data stored on it, Nero can erase it prior to burning the disc.)
3. Start the StartSmart menu.
4. Click the **Photo and Video** category.
5. Click **Convert DVD-Video Movies to Nero Digital**. The Nero Recode window appears.
6. Click **Import Titles**. An Import Title dialog box appears, as shown in Figure 5-2.

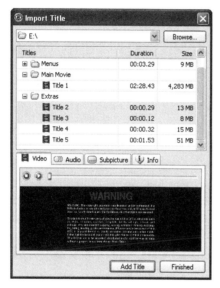

Figure 5-2: The Import Title dialog box lets you choose which parts (titles) of a DVD you want to copy

7. Click the video file that you want to copy. (To select more than one video file, hold down the CTRL key and click each video file that you want to add. To select a range of video files, click the first file you want, hold down the SHIFT key, and click the last file you want. Nero selects the first and last files, along with every file in between.)
8. Click **Add Title**. Nero Recode adds your chosen files.
9. Click **Finished**. Nero Recode displays your chosen video files, as shown in Figure 5-3 on the next page.
10. (Optional.) Drag a video file up or down in the Nero Recode window to rearrange the order of your video files.
11. (Optional.) Drag the **Video Quality** slider left or right. Decreasing the video quality creates a smaller file.

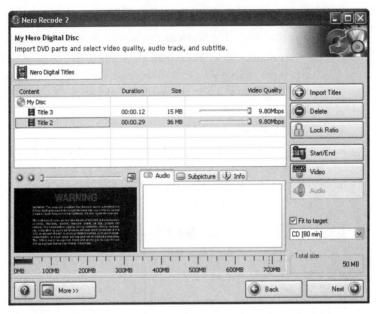

Figure 5-3: Nero Recode displays your chosen video files

12. (Optional.) Click a video file and click the **Lock Ratio** button. (The aspect ratio determines the vertical and horizontal size of a video file when it appears on a screen.)

13. (Optional.) Click the **Start/End** button. Nero displays a Set Start/End Frames dialog box, as shown in Figure 5-4. Drag the frame sliders until you see the frames you want to see first and last in the two panes. Click **OK**.

14. Make sure a check mark appears in the **Fit to target** check box.

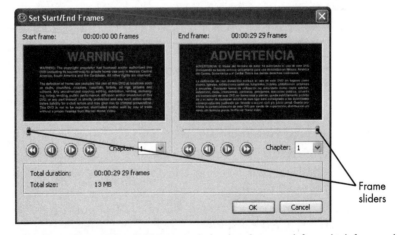

Figure 5-4: The Set Start/End Frames dialog box lets you define which frames should appear first and last in a video file

15. Click in the **Fit to target** list box and choose a destination for your video files, such as CD or DVD.

16. Click **Next**. Nero displays the burn settings, as shown in Figure 5-5.

Figure 5-5: Nero displays the burn settings for your chosen video files

17. Click in the **Destination** list box and choose the CD or DVD rewritable drive where you inserted a blank CD or DVD.

18. Click the **Burn** button. (Nero may display a dialog box informing you that you can improve the video quality of your video files if you encode your files again. You can select some or all of your video files to encode, and then click **OK**.) When the burning is done, a dialog box appears, asking whether you want to save a log file of the burn process.

19. Click **Yes** or **No**.

20. Click **Next** and then click **Exit**. The StartSmart menu appears again.

Creating a VCD or Super VCD

Basically, a VCD is just an ordinary CD that contains video instead of data or music. The Super VCD standard is a new and different format that stores more video at better quality on an ordinary CD. Although they are not as well known as the DVD format, VCD and Super VCD are two video formats for storing and playing video on ordinary CDs.

Philips and Sony introduced the VCD standard in 1993, but most countries had already adopted video cassette recorders (VCRs) instead. However, the VCD format became popular in Asia, which had yet to adopt VCRs. As a result, VCD players are nearly as common in Asia as VCRs are in North America. Because a single VCD can hold only approximately 70 minutes of video, most full-length movies require two VCDs with VCDs offering video quality similar to video cassettes. Curiously, one of the most popular uses for VCDs has been in karaoke players.

When the rest of the world began abandoning VCRs to adopt the newer DVD format, the Chinese government ignored it for economic and political reasons. Economically, DVD players and discs cost much more than ordinary CD equipment. Politically, the DVD format was controlled by the DVD Consortium, a collection of non-Asian corporations that demanded royalty payments from every manufacturer of DVD players. Not wanting to adopt an expensive video format that required royalty payments, the Chinese government backed the Super VCD standard instead. While still not as popular in the rest of the world as in Asia, the Super VCD standard can still be useful for storing video on ordinary CDs inexpensively.

Super VCD provides better video quality than VCD, but despite its name, Super VCD is not a superset of the VCD standard but an entirely different standard instead. As a result, you probably won't be able to play a Super VCD disc in a VCD player.

To create a VCD or Super VCD, follow these steps:

1. Start the StartSmart menu.

2. Insert a blank CD into your rewritable CD or DVD drive.

3. Click the CD tab in the upper-right corner of the StartSmart menu. (If you don't have a rewritable DVD drive, you may not see a CD tab in the right corner.)

4. Click the **Photo and Video** category.

5. Click **Make Video CD** or **Make Super Video CD**. The NeroVision Express window appears.

6. Click **Add Video Files**. An Open dialog box appears.

7. Click on the video file you want to add. (To select more than one video file, hold down the CTRL key and click each video file that you want to add. To select a range of video files, click the first file you want, hold down the SHIFT key, and click the last file you want. Nero selects the first and last file, along with every file in between.)

8. Click **Open**. NeroVision Express displays your video files.

9. (Optional.) Drag a video file up or down in the list to change the order of the files.

10. Click **Next**. NeroVision Express shows you what the opening screen looks like, as shown in Figure 5-6.

Figure 5-6: NeroVision Express creates an opening screen for your VCD or Super VCD

11. If you want to change any part of the opening screen, such as the background or text, click the item you want to change, such as **Shadow** or **Layout**. When you are done, click **Next**.

12. Click **Next**. NeroVision Express previews your opening screen with a remote control so you can test it out.

13. Click **Next**. NeroVision Express displays the burn options, as shown in Figure 5-7.

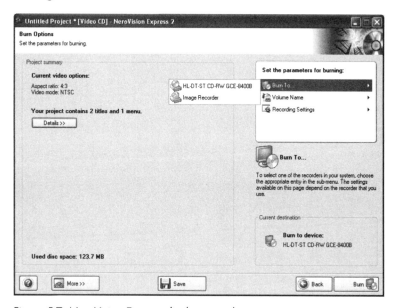

Figure 5-7: NeroVision Express displays your burn settings

14. Click **Burn To** and click the drive where you want to burn your video files.
15. Click the **Burn** button.

Once Nero finishes burning your VCD or Super VCD, you can play it back using the Nero ShowTime program, as described in Chapter 9.

6

DESIGNING CD AND DVD
LABELS AND COVERS

Once you burn photographs, music, or video to a CD or DVD, you may want to take one final step and design your own labels and covers for your creations. Not only will this give your discs a professional look, but it will help identify what's on each particular disc.

To help you design CD and DVD labels and covers, Nero comes with the Nero Cover Designer program, which works like a desktop publishing program where you can type text, add graphics, and arrange the whole thing to look pretty.

A label fits directly onto a CD or DVD and stays in place with glue. A cover folds up and fits inside or around the different types of plastic disc cases. Nero can even help you design labels and covers with the same background and graphic style so your entire CD or DVD package looks consistent and professional.

Starting Nero Cover Designer

To start the Nero Cover Designer program, follow these steps:

1. Start the StartSmart menu.
2. Click the **Extras** category.
3. Click **Make Label or Cover**. The Nero Cover Designer window appears and displays a New Document dialog box, as shown in Figure 6-1.

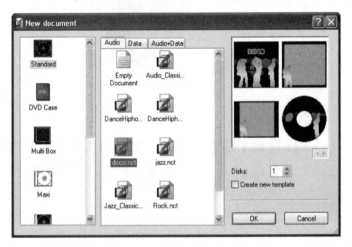

Figure 6-1: The New Document dialog box lets you choose a template for creating a new CD or DVD label or cover

4. Click the type of disc you want to create a label or cover for (such as **Standard** or **Mini CD**). If you click **Standard**, Nero displays sample templates you can use.
5. Click the tab that represents the type of data on the disc, such as **Audio**, **Data**, or **Audio+Data**.
6. Click a template to use, and click **OK**. If you don't want to use a template, click the **Empty Document** icon, click **OK**, and Nero Cover Designer will display a blank document or a template. From here, you can add text and graphics or change the background images and colors that appear on every part of your cover and label.

NOTE *Depending on the type of disc you choose in step 4, Nero Cover Designer may display from one to four tabs near the bottom-left corner of the window. When designing a Standard CD or DVD cover or label, Nero Cover Designer displays four tabs that represent the front cover of the disc case, the back cover of the disc case, the inlay, which rests underneath the disc in its case, and the actual label that appears on the disc itself.*

Changing the Background

The simplest way to modify the appearance of your cover and label is to change the color or image that appears in the background. If you are creating a front and back cover and a disc label, you can set the background colors or images on each part separately. That way your disc label can display one color or image, and the front cover of your disc case can display a different color or image.

Changing the Background Color

To change the background color of your cover or label, follow these steps:

1. In the bottom-left corner of the Nero Cover Designer window, as shown in Figure 6-2, click the tab that represents the part of your cover (such as **Front** or **Rear**) that you want to modify.

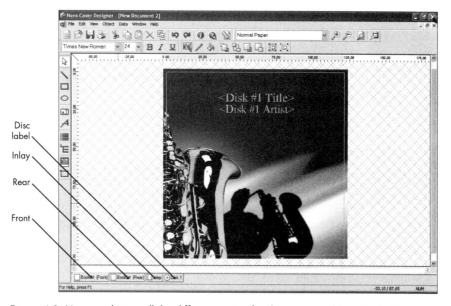

Figure 6-2: You can design all the different parts of a disc cover within a single Nero Designer window

2. Click the **Object** menu, and click **Background Properties**. A Background Properties dialog box appears.

3. Click the **Brush** tab to display the color wheel, as shown in Figure 6-3 on the next page. (If the color wheel appears gray, click the button that displays a big black **X** in the center.)

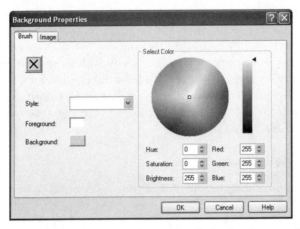

Figure 6-3: The Background Properties dialog box lets you choose colors or images to appear in the background

4. Click in the **Style** list box, and choose a style pattern, such as a solid color or diagonal line pattern.

5. Click a color in the color wheel to choose a color or drag the slider, up or down, to the right of the color wheel. As an alternative, change the values of the **Hue**, **Saturation**, **Brightness**, **Red**, **Blue**, or **Green** text boxes to define a color more precisely.

6. Click **OK**. Your chosen color appears as the background for your cover or label.

Changing the Background Image

Rather than use a solid color or pattern of colors, you may want to display an image on your cover or label instead. Take care that the image isn't so dark or so light that it prevents you from seeing any additional text or graphics you may want to add later.

To add a background image, follow these steps:

1. In the bottom-left corner of the Nero Cover Designer window, click the tab that represents the part of your cover (such as **Front** or **Rear**) that you want to modify.

2. Click the **Object** menu, and click **Background Properties**. A Background Properties dialog box appears.

3. Click the **Image** tab.

4. Click the **File** button. An Open dialog box appears. (If you click **TWAIN**, you can import an image from a scanner.)

5. Click the image you want to use, and then click **Open**. The Background Properties dialog box displays your chosen image, as shown in Figure 6-4.

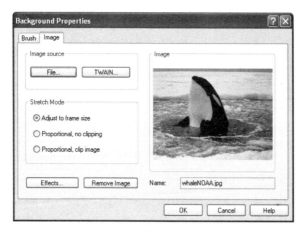

Figure 6-4: The Background Properties dialog box displays your image and gives you options for modifying its appearance

6. Click one of the following radio buttons in the Stretch Mode group:

Adjust to frame size   Expands or shrinks your image to fit completely in the background, but it may stretch your image unnaturally

Proportional, no clipping   Displays your image without expanding or shrinking it at all, which may either cut off part of the image or leave exposed areas of the cover or label that the image doesn't cover up

Proportional, clip image   Expands your image to fill the entire background while keeping its width and height proportions the same

7. Click the **Effects** button. A pop-up menu appears, giving you options to modify the appearance of your image, such as brightening or twisting it into odd shapes.

8. Click **OK** when you are finished adjusting the image.

If you want to remove an image from the background, follow these steps:

1. In the bottom-left corner of the Nero Cover Designer window, click the tab that represents the part of your cover (such as **Front** or **Rear**) that you want to modify.

2. Click the **Object** menu, and click **Background Properties**. A Background Properties dialog box appears.

3. Click the **Image** tab.

4. Click the **Remove Image** button. Nero Cover Designer removes the image from the Background Properties dialog box.

5. Click **OK.**

Playing with Text

Nero Cover Designer lets you place three types of text on a cover or label:

- Plain, ordinary text that resembles anything you might type in a word processor
- Artistic text, which you can rotate into different positions
- Fields, which contain data such as the names of individual songs or album titles

Typing Ordinary Text

The main difference between ordinary text and artistic text is that Nero can bend artistic text into curves, while ordinary text simply appears trapped within the confines of a box. To put ordinary text on a label or cover, follow these steps:

1. In the bottom-left corner of the Nero Cover Designer window, click the tab that represents the part of your cover (such as **Front** or **Rear**) that you want to modify.
2. Click the **Text Box tool**, as shown in Figure 6-5. The mouse pointer turns into a crosshair.

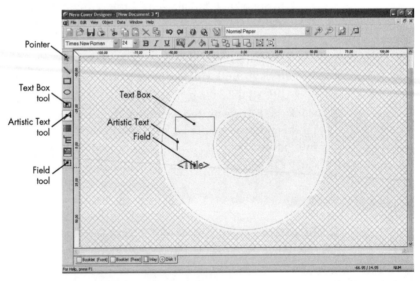

Figure 6-5: Nero lets you add three different types of text to a cover or label

3. Move the mouse pointer over the disc label or cover, and click and drag the mouse to draw a rectangle. Nero displays a text box with black handles around it.
4. Double-click the text box. Nero displays the Properties dialog box, as shown in Figure 6-6.

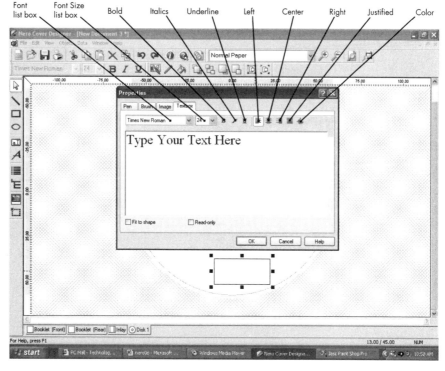

Figure 6-6: The Properties dialog box lets you type text and choose fonts, colors, and font styles

5. Type your text in the text box of the Properties dialog box.

6. (Optional.) Click in the **Font** list box, and choose a font to display your text.

7. (Optional.) Click in the **Font Size** list box, and choose a size for your text, such as **24** or **48**.

8. (Optional.) Click the **Bold, Italics**, or **Underline** buttons to bold, italicize, or underline your text.

9. (Optional.) Click the **Left, Center, Right**, or **Justified** alignment icons to align your text.

10. (Optional.) Click the **Color** icon, and choose a color for your text. If you have already typed some text, highlight it first and then click a color.

11. (Optional.) Click the **Image** tab, and click **File** or **TWAIN** to add an image inside your text box. Make sure your image isn't too dark or bright, or it might make your text hard to read.

12. Click **OK**. Nero displays your text inside the text box that you created in step 5.

To edit text that you already created, follow these steps:

1. Click the **Pointer** tool.
2. Double-click the text box that contains the text you want to edit. The Properties dialog box appears, and you can edit text, change colors or font sizes, and so on.
3. Click **OK** when you're finished.

Creating Artistic Text

Unlike ordinary text, artistic text can bend and appear with different colored patterns inside each letter. To create artistic text, follow these steps:

1. In the bottom-left corner of the Nero Cover Designer window, click the tab that represents the part of your cover (such as **Front** or **Rear**) that you want to modify.
2. Click the **Artistic Text** tool.
3. Click the cover or label where you want your text to appear.
4. Type your text, and press ENTER when you're finished. Nero displays your artistic text outlined with black handles around it.
5. Click the **Pointer** tool.
6. Double-click the artistic text you just created. A Properties dialog box appears, as shown in Figure 6-7.

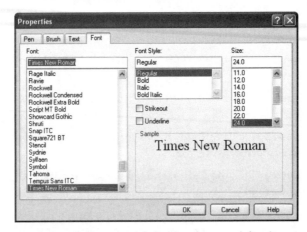

Figure 6-7: The Properties dialog box lets you define how your artistic text appears

7. (Optional.) Click in the **Font**, **Font Style**, and **Size** list boxes to modify the appearance of your text.
8. (Optional.) Click the **Strikeout** or **Underline** check boxes.
9. Click **OK.**

Editing Artistic Text

You may want to edit artistic text after you've created it. To edit artistic text, follow these steps:

1. Click the **Pointer** tool, and double-click the artistic text that you want to edit. The Properties dialog box appears.
2. Click the **Text** tab, and click in the **Content** text box.
3. Edit your text.
4. Click **OK.**

Coloring Artistic Text

Artistic text can appear with different patterns or colors inside each letter. However, if you choose a particular pattern or color for your artistic text, it changes the color for all the letters of your artistic text. To color artistic text, follow these steps:

1. Click the **Pointer** tool and double-click the artistic text that you want to color. The Properties dialog box appears.
2. Click the **Brush** tab, as shown in Figure 6-8.

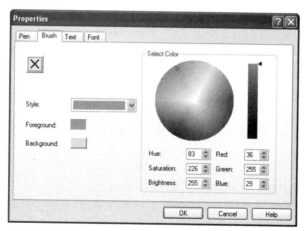

Figure 6-8: The Brush tab lets you choose a color and pattern to display inside the letters of your artistic text

3. Click in the **Style** list box, and choose a pattern.
4. Click in the **Foreground** box, and then click a color from the color wheel. (To choose a precise color, you can also type specific values into the **Hue**, **Saturation**, **Brightness**, **Red**, **Green**, and **Blue** text boxes.)
5. Click **OK.**

Changing the Pen Width for Artistic Text

When you create artistic text, Nero displays your text so each letter is hollow inside, and you can fill them with a pattern or color, as explained in the previous "Coloring Artistic Text" section. However, to further modify the appearance of artistic text, you can also change the pen width, which defines the thickness of the lines that outline each letter.

To change the pen width, follow these steps:

1. Click the **Pointer** tool, and double-click the artistic text whose pen width you want to change. The Properties dialog box appears.
2. Click the **Pen** tab to display the current width and color used to outline the letters of your artistic text, as shown in Figure 6-9.

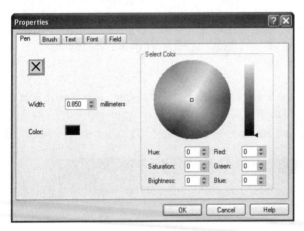

Figure 6-9: The Pen tab lets you change the color and width of the lines that outline your artistic text

3. Click the up or down arrows of the **Width** box to set a new width.
4. Click in the **Color** box, and click a color in the color wheel. (As an alternative, you can type a specific value in the **Hue**, **Saturation**, **Brightness**, **Red**, **Green**, or **Blue** boxes to define a specific color.)
5. Click **OK.** Nero displays your artistic text with the new pen width and color.

Bending Artistic Text

You can bend artistic text so the text follows a curve, which can be useful for displaying text around the curved edges of a disc. To bend artistic text, follow these steps:

1. Click the **Pointer** tool, and double-click the artistic text that you want to bend. The Properties dialog box appears.
2. Click the **Text** tab, and click the **Bent** check box to bend your text.

3. Click **OK**. Nero displays your artistic text bent into a curve with a center point that appears as a circle with a crosshair inside of it, as shown in Figure 6-10.

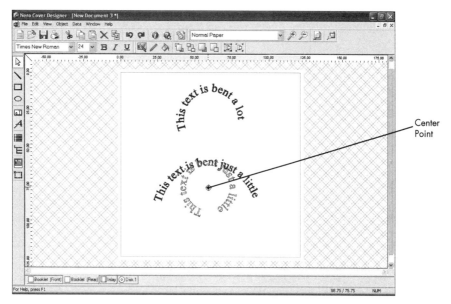

Figure 6-10: By dragging the center point closer to the artistic text, you can make it bend more

4. Move the mouse pointer over the center point, and click and drag it closer or farther away from your artistic text to bend it into the shape that you want.

Playing with Fields

With both ordinary and artistic text, you have to type exactly what you want to appear every time. When you create a field, you just have to type the text in once, and Nero automatically types that text in your field no matter how many places you put that field on your cover or label.

Fields are typically used to store song titles or album names so that you just have to type that information once and Nero can display it everywhere you want without you having to type it over and over again.

To add a field to a cover or label, follow these steps:

1. In the bottom-left corner of the Nero Cover Designer window, click the tab that represents the part of your cover (such as **Front** or **Rear**) that you want to modify.

2. Click the **Field** tool. A pop-up menu appears listing the types of data you can display in a field, as shown in Figure 6-11 on the next page.

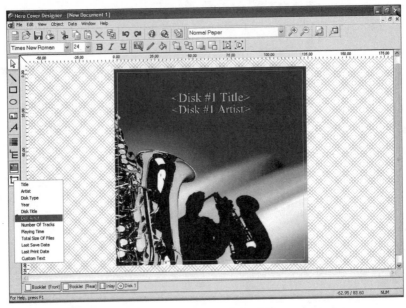

Figure 6-11: The Field tool pop-up menu lists all the different types of data you can choose to store and display in your newly created field

3. Click the type of field you want to display on your cover or label, such as **Disk Title** or **Number of Tracks**. Nero displays your chosen field within angle brackets, such as <Title>.

Typing Data into a Field

Once you've added some fields to your cover or label, you need to define the data you want in each field, such as the title or recording artist. That way, if you have two Title fields, Nero can display the same information in each Title field, whether it appears on the front or back cover or on the disc label.

To enter and edit the data that will appear in your fields, follow these steps:

1. Click the **Data** menu, and choose **Document Data**. Nero displays a Document Data dialog box, as shown in Figure 6-12. The Document Data dialog box displays four items in a hierarchical tree at the left, along with the type of fields you can edit in each one at the right:

   Document Allows you to specify the title, year of release, and artist/publisher

   Disk Allows you to specify the subtitle, type (audio, data, or audio+data), and artist/publisher

   Audio or file system data Offers no editable fields, but provides buttons to add audio tracks or data files.

   Audio track or file data Allows you to specify the title, artist, playing time, and extended info

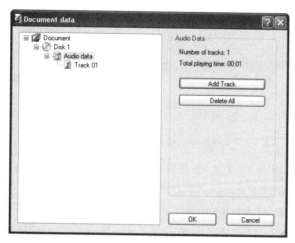

Figure 6-12: The Document Data dialog box lets you store information that you want Nero to display automatically in a field

2. Click the **Document**, **Disk**, **Audio data** or **Track** icon to edit the fields, as shown in Figure 6-13.

NOTE *If you click the **Apply to all subitems** button for the Document or Disk icons, Nero automatically includes the same text in any duplicate fields displayed. So if you type "Britney Spears" in the Title field of the Document icon and click the **Apply to all subitems** button, the name Britney Spears will also appear in the Title field when you display the Document fields.*

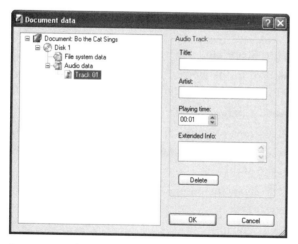

Figure 6-13: The Audio Track group lets you type data into the Title, Artist, Playing Time, and Extended Info fields

3. Click **OK**. If you typed any text in the fields you added to your cover or label, Nero displays that text on your cover or label. Instead of seeing something like <Title> on your label, you'll see the actual title text you typed, such as "The White Album."

Editing the Appearance of a Field

Although you can only edit the text displayed in a field by choosing the **Document Data** command under the **Data** menu, you can change the text's font, color, or even add leading text (which appears in front of your field) or trailing text (which appears after your field) by changing the field's properties.

To edit the appearance of a field, follow these steps:

1. Click the **Pointer** tool.
2. Double-click the field that you want to modify. The Properties dialog box appears, as shown in Figure 6-14.

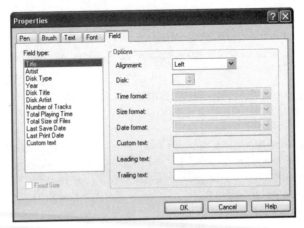

Figure 6-14: The Properties dialog box lets you modify the appearance of your fields, such as changing the alignment or adding leading or trailing text

3. Click the appropriate tab for the options you want to change:

   Field Modifies the alignment of a field or changes the format a field uses to display data such as the time or a date

   Font Changes the font of the text in a field

   Text Lets you bend or straighten the appearance of a field

   Brush Lets you choose a color and pattern to appear inside the letters of text in a field

   Pen Lets you change the color and width of lines that make up your letters

4. Click **OK** when you're finished.

Playing with Graphics

To make your disc covers and labels pretty, you can import graphics captured by a digital camera or scanner, or created with a graphics program, such as Photoshop or CorelDraw.

To add graphics to a cover or label, follow these steps:

1. In the bottom-left corner of the Nero Cover Designer window, click the tab that represents the part of your cover (such as **Front** or **Rear**) that you want to modify.

2. Click the **Image** tool. An Open dialog box appears, as shown in Figure 6-15.

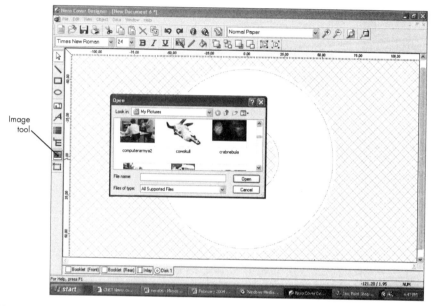

Figure 6-15: The Open dialog box lets you view your graphic files so you can see which one you want

3. Click the graphic image you want to use, and click **Open**. Nero displays a box that moves with the mouse pointer.

4. Click the mouse where you want to insert your graphic image.

To add special graphic effects to your image, follow these steps:

1. Click the **Pointer** tool.

2. Double-click the graphic image that you want to modify. A Properties dialog box appears.

3. Click the **Effects** button. A pop-up menu appears.

4. Click the effect you want, such as **Filters** or **Rotate**. Depending on which effect you choose, Nero displays a different dialog box in which you can set the details for the effect.

> **Adjust**   Alters the visual appearance of a graphic image, such as its brightness or contrast
>
> **Flip**   Changes the position of your graphic image horizontally or vertically

Filters   Alters your graphic image as if viewed through a different visual effect, such as making an image appear to be made out of individual tiles put together

Negate   Displays your graphic image like a photographic negative where light areas appear dark and dark areas appear light

Pinch   Squeezes or expands the middle of your graphic image

Rotate   Spins your image around left or rotate by 0–270 degrees

Swirl   Makes your image look like it's twisting around as if flowing clockwise or counterclockwise down a drain, as shown in Figure 6-16

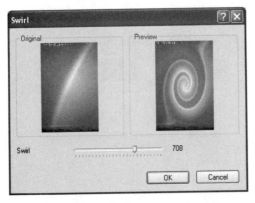

Figure 6-16: The Swirl effect is one of many ways to modify the appearance of a graphic image

5.   Click **OK** when you're finished.

Moving, Resizing, and Deleting Text and Graphics

Once you've placed text and graphics on your label or cover, you may want to move, resize, or delete them at a later date. If you ever move, resize, or delete text or graphics and change your mind, just press **CTRL+Z** to undo your last change.

Moving Text and Graphics

Nero offers two ways to move text and graphics:

- Drag the text or graphic with the mouse
- Type exact coordinates for your text or graphic

To move text or graphics quickly with the mouse, follow these steps:

1.   Click the **Pointer** tool.

2. Click the text or graphic that you want to move. Nero displays black handles around your chosen text or graphic. (If you want to move two or more text or graphic boxes at the same time, hold down the **SHIFT** key and click any additional text or graphic boxes.)

3. Click the text or graphic box, and drag the mouse to move the text or graphic to a new location.

4. Release the mouse button when you're happy with the new location of your text or graphic.

To type in specific coordinates for text or graphics, follow these steps:

1. Click the **Pointer** tool.

2. Click the text or graphic that you want to move. Nero displays black handles around your chosen text or graphic.

3. Click the **Object** menu, and click **Geometry**, or press **ALT+G**. The Geometry dialog box appears, as shown in Figure 6-17.

Figure 6-17: The Geometry dialog box lets you type the specific X and Y position for the upper-left corner of your text or graphic

4. Type a value in the **X** and **Y** position text boxes, and click **OK**.

Aligning Text and Graphics

Another way to move text or graphics is with the Align command, which aligns your selected text or graphics with the top, bottom, left, or right edges of your cover or label. To align text or graphics, follow these steps:

1. Click the **Pointer** tool.

2. Click the text or graphic that you want to move. Nero displays black handles around your chosen text or graphic.

3. Click the **Object** menu, and click **Align**. An Align Elements dialog box appears, as shown in Figure 6-18 on the next page.

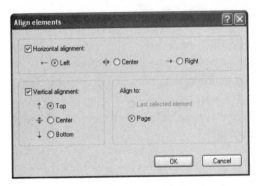

Figure 6-18: The Align elements dialog box lets you quickly position a graphic image on your disc cover or label

4. Click the **Left**, **Center**, or **Right** radio button in the Horizontal alignment group.

5. Click the **Top**, **Center**, or **Bottom** radio button in the Vertical alignment group.

6. Click **OK**. Nero aligns your text or graphic.

Overlapping Text or Graphics

If you place two or more text or graphic boxes so they overlap each other, one will cover part of the other, as shown in Figure 6-19.

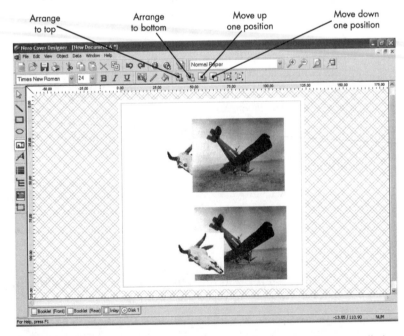

Figure 6-19: When two text or graphic boxes overlap one another, one will always cover part of the other

To rearrange the way text and graphics overlap one another, follow these steps:

1. Click the **Pointer** tool.
2. Click the text or graphic that you want to arrange. Nero displays black handles around your chosen text or graphic.
3. Click an icon, such as **Arrange to top**. As an alternative, click the **Object** menu, click **Arrange**, and then click one of the following commands (equivalent icon commands appear in parentheses below):

> **To Top (Arrange to top icon)**   Moves your selected text or graphic box to the top, so it overlaps anything underneath
>
> **To Bottom (Arrange to bottom icon)**   Moves your selected text or graphic box underneath, so anything else may overlap it
>
> **Move Up (Move up one position icon)**   Moves your selected text or graphic box one layer closer to the top
>
> **Move Down (Move down one position icon)**   Moves your selected text or graphic box one layer closer to the bottom

Resizing Text or Graphics

Nero offers two ways to resize text and graphics:

- Drag a corner or edge of the text or graphic with the mouse
- Type exact coordinates for your text or graphic

To resize text or graphics quickly with the mouse, follow these steps:

1. Click the **Pointer** tool.
2. Click the text or graphic that you want to resize. Nero displays black handles around your chosen text or graphic.
3. Move the mouse pointer over a black handle on the edge or corner of your selected text or graphic.
4. Click the edge or corner, and drag the mouse to resize the text or graphic to a new size.
5. Release the mouse button when you're happy with the new size of your text or graphic.

To type in specific height and width dimension for text or graphics, follow these steps:

1. Click the **Pointer** tool.
2. Click the text or graphic that you want to resize. Nero displays black handles around your chosen text or graphic.

3. Click the **Object** menu, and click **Geometry**, or press **ALT+G**. The Geometry dialog box appears (see Figure 6-17 on page 95).

4. Type a value in the **Width** and **Height** text boxes, and click **OK**.

Deleting Text or Graphics

If you typed some text or added some graphics and later decide you don't want them, you can delete them by following these steps:

1. Click the **Pointer** tool.

2. Click the text or graphics that you want to delete. Nero displays black handles around your chosen text or graphic. (To select multiple text or graphic boxes, hold down the **SHIFT** key and then click each additional text or graphic box.)

3. Press **DELETE**. Nero deletes your chosen text or graphic.

Printing

Once you're finished designing your disc covers and label, you'll want to print them out so you can use them. To print disc labels, you'll need special disc-label paper, and you'll need to learn which way to insert the paper into your printer so it prints correctly. (Try printing out your design on ordinary paper first, so you don't waste your special disc-label paper figuring out the correct way to feed it into your printer.)

Defining Your Paper Stock

Before you start printing, you have to tell Nero what type of paper you're using. To define your paper stock, follow these steps:

1. Click the **File** menu, and click **Paper Stocks**. A Paper Stocks dialog box appears, as shown in Figure 6-20.

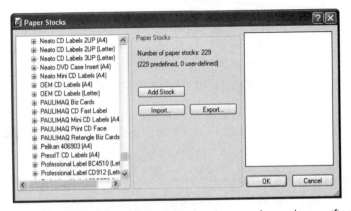

Figure 6-20: The Paper Stocks dialog box lets you choose the specific type of disc-label and cover paper your printer uses

2. Click the name of the paper stock you're using.

3. Click **OK.**

Calibrating Your Printer

After telling Nero what type of paper stock you're using, you should also take time to calibrate your printer. Because every printer is slightly different, calibration simply lets you print out a test page and tell Nero how to adjust your printer so your covers and labels print accurately on your paper stock every time.

NOTE *You may need to recalibrate your printer each time you replace an ink cartridge because replacement ink cartridges won't be in the exact position as the previous ink cartridge that it replaced.*

To calibrate your printer, follow these steps:

1. Click the **File** menu, and click **Preferences**. An Application Preferences dialog box appears.

2. Click the **Printing** tab, as shown in Figure 6-21.

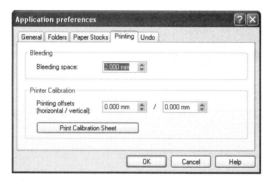

Figure 6-21: The Printing tab of the Application Preferences dialog box lets you print a calibration sheet

3. Turn on your printer, insert an ordinary sheet of paper, and click **Print Calibration Sheet**.

4. Follow the instructions printed on the calibration sheet. (Fold the printed calibration sheet in half horizontally and vertically, and then determine where the two creases intersect the axes printed on the sheet.)

5. Repeat steps 1 and 2 to display the **Printing** tab of the Application Preferences sheet.

6. Type the values from the folded calibration sheet into the **Printing offsets** boxes in the Printer Calibration group.

7. Click **OK.**

Previewing and Printing

Once you've defined your paper stock and calibrated your printer, you're ready to start printing. Because special disc-label and cover paper can be expensive, it's a good idea to preview your cover and label before you actually print them.

To see a print preview of your cover and labels, follow these steps:

1. Click the **File** menu, and click **Print Preview**. The Print Preview dialog box appears, as shown in Figure 6-22.

Figure 6-22: The Print Preview dialog box shows you what your final cover and label will look like when printed out

2. Click the **Prev Page** or **Next Page** buttons if necessary to see your entire cover and label design.
3. If you're happy with how it looks, turn on your printer, insert your special disc-label and cover paper, and click **Print**.

7

EDITING SOUND

Once you've either recorded, created, or copied an audio file to your hard disk, you may want to alter the way it sounds by adjusting the volume, splitting the audio track into parts, adding special audio effects, and so on. Nero lets you edit audio files and then save your work in a variety of different file formats. With Nero's audio editing capabilities, you can give any recording a crisp, clean sound that can rival anything a commercial audio CD might offer.

Running Nero Wave Editor

The Nero program that lets you edit audio files is called Nero Wave Editor. To run Nero Wave Editor, follow these steps:

1. Start the StartSmart menu.
2. Click the **Standard Mode** button to switch to expert mode.
3. Click the **Audio** category.
4. Click **Edit Audio**. The Nero Wave Editor window appears.
5. Click the **File** menu and click **Open** (or press CTRL+O or click the **Open** icon). An Open dialog box appears.
6. Click the digital audio file that you want to edit, and click **Open**. The Nero Wave Editor loads your chosen audio file, as shown in Figure 7-1.

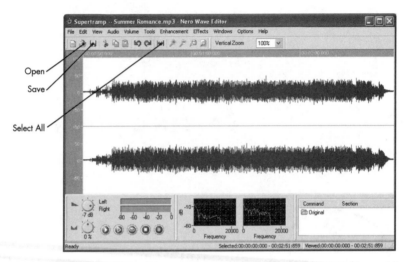

Figure 7-1: The Nero Wave Editor displays your audio file as a series of jagged lines that represent sounds

Adjusting the Volume

The Nero Wave Editor offers several different ways to alter the volume of a digital audio file:

- Raise or lower the volume of an individual audio file
- Mute part of an audio file
- Normalize multiple audio files
- Fade the sound in and out

Raising and Lowering the Volume of a Digital Audio File

One common problem with audio files is that the volume may be too high or too low compared to other audio files. To fix the volume of an audio file, follow these steps:

1. Follow the steps in the earlier "Running Nero Wave Editor" section to load the audio file you want to edit.

2. Click the **Edit** menu and click **Select All** (or press **CTRL+A** or click the **Select All** icon). Nero highlights your entire audio file. (If you click in the middle of an audio file and drag the mouse or press the left or right arrow keys, you can highlight just part of your audio file.)

3. Click the **Volume** menu and click **Volume Change**. A Volume Change dialog box appears, as shown in Figure 7-2.

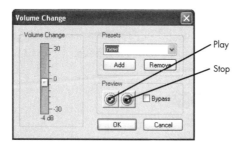

Figure 7-2: The Volume Change dialog box lets you adjust the volume and hear the results

4. Click **Play**.

5. Drag the **Volume Change** slider up or down to modify the volume until you like the way it sounds.

6. Click **OK** when you're happy with the volume of your digital audio file.

7. Click the **File** menu and click **Save** (or press **CTRL+S** or click the **Save** icon). Or, if you want to save your digital audio file under another name, click the **Save As** command instead.

Muting Part of an Audio File

Another way to modify an audio file is to mute part of the file, such as the beginning or end, which may contain unwanted noise. To mute part of an audio file, follow these steps:

1. Follow the steps in the earlier "Running Nero Wave Editor" section to load the audio file you want to edit.

2. Click the part of the audio file that you want to mute. Nero displays a vertical line. You can adjust the position of this vertical line by pressing the left or right arrow keys.

3. Click and drag the mouse, or hold down the **SHIFT** key while pressing the left or right arrow key, to select part of your audio file.

4. Click in the **Volume** menu and click **Mute**. Nero displays the selected part of your audio file as a flat line.

Normalizing Multiple Audio Files

If you play several different audio files, you may find that some were recorded at higher or lower volumes than others, which means you may need to constantly adjust the volume to hear one song and then turn down the volume to avoid getting blasted out of your chair by the next song. To fix this problem, you can normalize the volume of an audio file so it matches the volume of your other digital audio files.

To normalize a digital audio file, follow these steps:

1. Follow the steps in the earlier "Running Nero Wave Editor" section to load the audio file you want to normalize.
2. Click the **Edit** menu and click **Select All** (or press **CTRL+A** or click the **Select All** icon). Nero highlights your entire audio file.
3. Click the **Volume** menu and click **Normalize**. A Normalize dialog box appears, as shown in Figure 7-3.

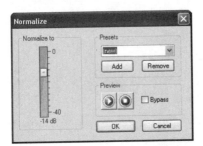

Figure 7-3: The Normalize dialog box lets you adjust the volume of an audio file

4. Drag the **Normalize to** slider up or down, and click the **Play** button to hear how your audio file sounds at your chosen volume.
5. Click **Stop** when you're happy with the way your audio file sounds.
6. (Optional.) Click in the **Presets** list box, and type a descriptive name to save your volume setting under. By saving your volume setting, you can later apply these same settings to another audio file by simply clicking this descriptive name instead of adjusting the **Normalize to** slider manually. Click the **Add** button to store your settings.
7. Click **OK**. At this point, you can save your audio file to preserve the changes you made.

Fading In and Out

Another way to adjust the volume of part of an audio file is to make the sound fade in or out, as is sometimes done at the beginning or end of a song. Nero offers four different ways to fade the sound:

Linear   The volume fades in or out at a rate proportional to the time

Exponential   The volume changes in keeping with an exponential function

Logarithmic   The volume changes in keeping with a logarithmic function

Sinusoidal   The volume changes at an interval of half the wavelength of a sinusoidal function

If none of these descriptions makes any sense to you, just experiment with the different methods and see which you prefer.

To make the volume of an audio file fade in or out, follow these steps:

1. Follow the steps in the earlier "Running Nero Wave Editor" section to load the audio file you want to edit.

2. Click the part of the audio file that you want to modify. Nero displays a vertical line. You can adjust the position of this vertical line by pressing the left and right arrow keys.

3. Click and drag the mouse, or hold down the SHIFT key while pressing the left or right arrow key, to select part of your audio file.

4. Click the **Volume** menu and click **Fade in or Fade out**. A pop-up menu appears.

5. Click one of the options displayed in the pop-up menu, such as **Exponential** or **Sinusoidal**. Nero fades the sound in or out for the part of the audio file you selected in steps 2 and 3.

Physically Manipulating Your Audio Files

You can edit an audio file by deleting part of the file (to trim the beginning or end), splitting it into separate parts, or combining multiple audio files into a single file.

Deleting Parts of an Audio File

The most common reason for deleting part of an audio file is to trim the beginning or end. To delete part of an audio file, follow these steps:

1. Follow the steps in the earlier "Running Nero Wave Editor" section to load the audio file you want to edit.

2. Click the part of the audio file that you want to modify. Nero displays a vertical line. You can adjust the position of this vertical line by pressing the left and right arrow keys.

3. Click and drag the mouse, or hold down the SHIFT key while pressing the left or right arrow key, to select part of your audio file.

4. Click the **Edit** menu and click **Delete** (or press CTRL+DEL). Nero deletes your chosen part of the audio file.

NOTE *If you suddenly change your mind about deleting part of an audio file, click the* **Edit** *menu and choose* **Undo** *(or press* CTRL+Z*).*

Splitting an Audio File

If you captured music from a tape cassette or vinyl record, your digital audio file may well contain several songs smashed into a single file. In cases like these, you may want to split a single audio file into two or more parts so you can isolate each song in its own file.

Splitting an Audio File Manually

To split an audio file manually, follow these steps:

1. Follow the steps in the earlier "Running Nero Wave Editor" section to load the audio file you want to split.

2. Click the audio file close to where you want to split it. Nero displays a vertical line. You can adjust the position of this vertical line by pressing the left and right arrow keys.

3. Click and drag the mouse, or hold down the SHIFT key while pressing the left or right arrow key, to select the part of your audio file that you want to save as a separate file.

4. Click the **Audio** menu and click **Play section** (or press the SPACEBAR). Nero plays the highlighted part of your audio file so you can make sure you've highlighted the part of the audio file that you want to save as a separate file. (You may need to repeat steps 2 and 3 to correctly select the part of the file you want. To help you see where a particular song may start or end, click the **View** menu and click **Zoom In** or **Zoom Out**.)

5. Click the **Edit** menu and click **Cut** (or press CTRL+X). Nero deletes your selected part of the audio file. Or you can click the **Edit** menu and click **Copy** (or press CTRL+C) if you don't want to delete the selected section of the file.

6. Click in the **File** menu and click **New** (or press CTRL+N). Nero opens a blank Wave Editor window.

7. Click the **Edit** menu and click **Paste** (or press CTRL+V). Nero pastes the part of the audio file you cut or copied in step 5. You can now trim the start or end of your audio file (using the steps explained in the previous "Deleting Parts of an Audio File" section) or just continue and save your audio file under a new name by clicking the **File** menu and then clicking **Save As**.

Splitting an Audio File Automatically

To help automate the process of splitting up an audio file consisting of multiple songs, Nero offers a special pause-detection feature. The moment Nero finds a pause in an audio file, it assumes that this pause is the end of one audio track, so it automatically splits off that part of the audio file.

To use Nero's pause-detection feature, you must specify the sound level that indicates a pause (splitting live recordings is more difficult than splitting studio recordings, because live recordings often have people cheering between the songs), the minimum number of seconds a pause must last, and the minimum length of a song. You may need to experiment with different settings until you find what works for your audio file.

To use Nero's pause-detection feature, follow these steps:

1.   Follow the steps in the earlier "Running Nero Wave Editor" section to load the audio file you want to split.

2.   Click the **Edit** menu and click **Pause Detection**. A Pause Detection dialog box appears, as shown in Figure 7-4.

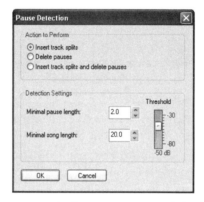

Figure 7-4: The Pause Detection dialog box lets you tell Nero how to recognize a legitimate pause in your audio file

3.   Click the **Insert track splits** radio button.

4.   Click in the **Minimal pause length** text box, and type a value or click the up and down arrows to specify a length of time.

5.   Click in the **Minimal song length** text box, and type a value or click the up and down arrows to specify the minimum length of a song.

6.   Drag the **Threshold** slider up or down to define the volume for a pause. (For live recordings, the threshold volume will be higher than for a studio recording.)

7.   Click **OK**. Nero displays red triangles to indicate the pauses in your audio file.

8.   Highlight each song, isolated by the red triangles, and follow steps 2–7 in the previous "Splitting an Audio File Manually" section.

Combining Multiple Audio Files

Sometimes you may have two or more separate audio files that you want to keep together so they play one after another. To combine multiple audio files into a single file, follow these steps:

1. Follow the steps in the earlier "Running Nero Wave Editor" section to load the first audio file that you want to combine.

2. Click the part of the audio file where you want to add the next audio file (such as at the beginning or end of the audio file you loaded in step 1). Nero displays a vertical line. You can adjust the position of this line by pressing the left or right arrow keys.

3. Click the **Edit** menu and click **Insert File**. An Open dialog box appears.

4. Click the audio file you want to add, and click **Open**. Nero adds your audio file.

5. Repeat steps 2–4 for each additional audio file you want to add.

When you combine audio files, there may be slight pauses where the files were joined. To delete these pauses automatically after you've combined your files, follow these steps:

1. Click the **Edit** menu and click **Pause Detection**. A Pause Detection dialog box appears (see Figure 7-4 on the previous page).

2. Click the **Delete pauses** radio button.

3. Click in the **Minimal pause length** text box, and type a value or click the up and down arrows to specify a length of time.

4. Click in the **Minimal song length** text box, and type a value or click the up and down arrows to specify the minimum length of a song.

5. Drag the **Threshold** slider up or down to define the volume for a pause. (For live recordings, the threshold volume will be higher than for a studio recording.)

6. Click **OK**. Nero removes the pauses and displays vertical dotted lines with the word "Cut" to show you where it removed pauses in your audio file. At this point you can save the changes (by pressing **CTRL+S**) or undo them (by pressing **CTRL+Z**).

Enhancing and Altering Sound

Once you've trimmed away the excess parts of an audio file, you may want to enhance or alter the way your digital audio files sound. Modifying audio files can take a lot of time and experimentation, but it allows you to turn mediocre recordings into crisp, clean sound or to create unique variations.

NOTE *Although most of Nero's special auditory enhancement features use technical terms that only an audio engineer might understand, you can just experiment with the different options on your own music to hear what these enhancements do.*

Nero organizes its different commands for modifying audio files into three different menus: Tools, Enhancements, and Effects. When you choose a command from the Tools, Enhancements, or Effects menu, Nero displays a green Play button and a blue Stop button so that way you can click the Play button to hear your audio file and then make various adjustments so you can hear how those adjustments affect the sound. If you don't like the way your changes have altered an audio file, click the blue **Stop** button and make new adjustments, or click the **Cancel** button. If you do like the way your altered audio file sounds, click the **OK** button to keep your changes and then click the **File** menu, and click **Save** to save your changes.

The Tools Menu Commands

The Tools menu offers commands for adjusting sound to improve the quality of an audio file. If you experiment with the Tools menu commands, you can also create odd audio effects such as slowing down an audio file so it sounds like a record player winding down. You can either use different tools on an entire audio file or just select parts of an audio file.

Stereo Processor Adjusts the sound through the left and right speakers, as shown in Figure 7-5.

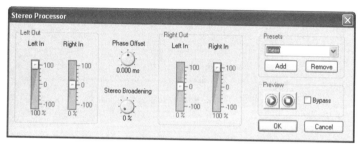

Figure 7-5: The Stereo Processor dialog box lets you adjust the stereo sound of an audio file

Dynamic Processor Adjusts the volume by dragging the points on a graph, as shown in Figure 7-6.

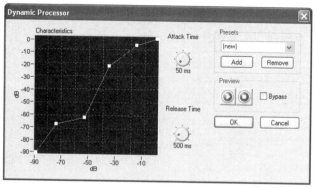

Figure 7-6: The Dynamic Processor dialog box lets you adjust the amplitude of an audio file

Equalizer   Provides a six-band equalizer to amplify or reset different frequency ranges, as shown in Figure 7-7.

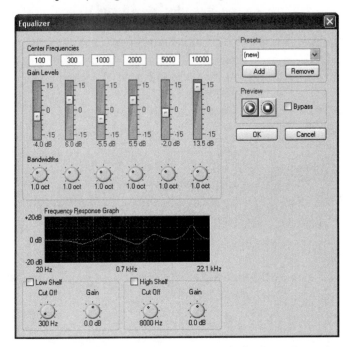

Figure 7-7: The Equalizer dialog box lets you adjust the different frequencies of an audio file

Transpose   Speeds up or slows down the tonality of an audio file (as shown in Figure 7-8) so voices sound high-pitched like a chipmunk's or low and deep like a record winding down.

Figure 7-8: The Transpose dialog box lets you adjust the tonality of an audio file

Time Correction   Speeds up or slows down the time scale of an audio file by a percentage, as shown in Figure 7-9.

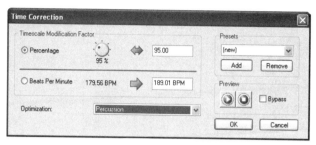

Figure 7-9: The Time Correction dialog box lets you adjust the time scale of an audio file

Karaoke Filter   Filters out sound that appears in both stereo channels (as shown in Figure 7-10), which is usually the vocals but can sometimes include other parts of a song as well.

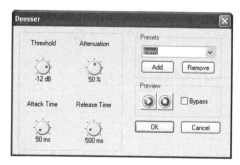

Figure 7-10: The Karaoke Filter dialog box lets you strip away vocals from an audio file

Deesser   Increases or decreases high-frequency "ess" sounds in an audio file, as shown in Figure 7-11.

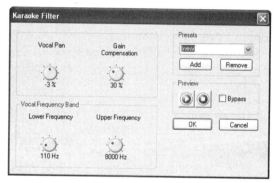

Figure 7-11: The Deesser dialog box lets you modify high frequencies of an audio file

Noise Gate Blocks sounds that drop below a preset level, as shown in Figure 7-12.

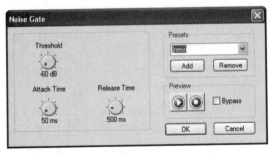

Figure 7-12: The Noise gate dialog box lets you block out sounds below a specified threshold

The Enhancements Menu Commands

The Enhancements menu offers commands for removing flaws from an audio file. Of course, if you alter these enhancements to a low or high extreme, you can make an audio file sound muffled or louder. You can either enhance an entire audio file or just select parts of an audio file.

Noise Reduction Reduces background noise, such as buzzing or tape hiss, as shown in Figure 7-13.

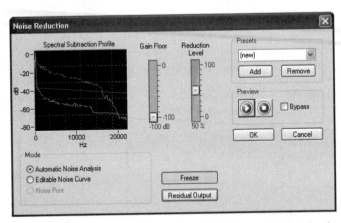

Figure 7-13: The Noise Reduction dialog box lets you remove background noise that may be interfering with the quality of your audio file

Band Extrapolation Synthesizes higher frequencies that produce artificial harmonics and low frequencies that produce powerful bass tones, as shown in Figure 7-14.

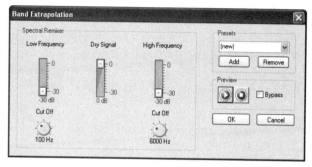

Figure 7-14: The Band Extrapolation dialog box lets you modify frequencies to improve the sound of a recording

Declicker   Removes clicks and pops, as shown in Figure 7-15, caused by scratches in audio files recorded from vinyl records.

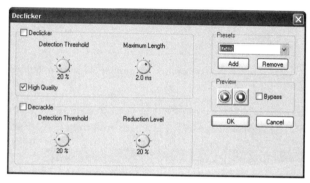

Figure 7-15: The Declicker dialog box lets you remove pops and clicks that may be interfering with the quality of your audio file

Filter Toolbox   Weeds out noise, such as buzzing, by providing low, high, and band pass filters, along with a user-defined frequency curve and three individual notch filters, as shown in Figure 7-16.

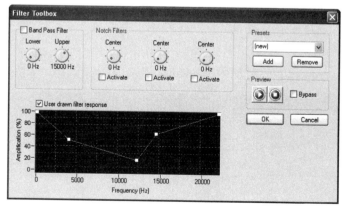

Figure 7-16: The Filter Toolbox dialog box provides various filters you can use to remove interference from an audio file

The Effects Menu Commands

The Effects menu provides commands for altering sound in an audio file that create new variations on that audio file, such as making the audio file sound like an echo or tweaking a singer's voice so it sounds high-pitched. You can either apply different effects to your entire audio file or just select parts of an audio file.

Chorus   Creates a chorus effect, as if more people were singing, as shown in Figure 7-17.

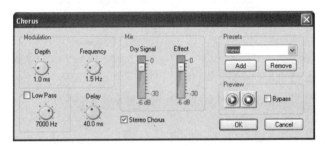

Figure 7-17: The Chorus dialog box lets you create the illusion that a chorus is singing instead of a single vocalist

Delay   Creates an echo effect in your audio file so that parts of your audio file repeat themselves after a short delay, as shown in Figure 7-18.

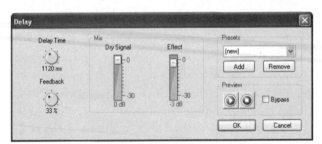

Figure 7-18: The Delay dialog box lets you define a delay time and feedback to create an echo within an audio file

Flanger   Mixes an audio file with a slightly delayed copy of itself, where the length of the delay constantly changes, as shown in Figure 7-19.

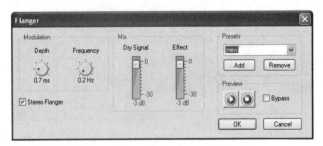

Figure 7-19: The Flanger dialog box can delay sound to create an echo effect

Reverb   Simulates sound reflecting off the walls of a large room, creating the illusion that the recording took place in a concert hall or stadium, as shown in Figure 7-20.

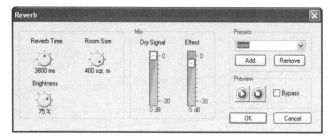

Figure 7-20: The Reverb dialog box lets you define a room size to mimic reverberation in your audio file

Wah-Wah   Modifies the tone by producing a high-end, treble-heavy tone to a deeper, muted sound, as shown in Figure 7-21.

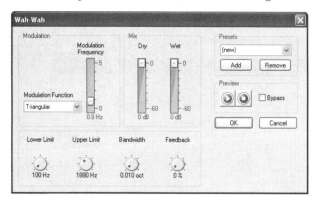

Figure 7-21: The Wah-Wah dialog box lets you alter the sound in your audio file

Voice Modification   Increases or deepens the vocals of a song so you can make any vocalist sound like they just inhaled a mouthful of helium, as shown in Figure 7-22.

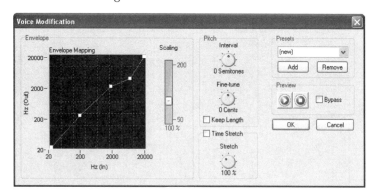

Figure 7-22: The Voice Modification dialog box lets you play with different frequencies in your audio file

Phaser Strengthens and weakens the harmonic components of an audio input signal and produces an output signal with a "floating" effect, as shown in Figure 7-23.

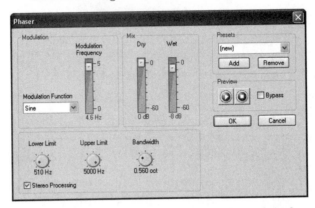

Figure 7-23: The Phaser dialog box lets you play with the frequencies in your audio file

Pitch Tuning Modifies the intonation of both vocal and instrumental recordings, as shown in Figure 7-24.

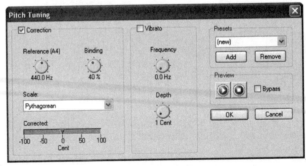

Figure 7-24: The Pitch Tuning dialog box lets you correct the intonation of your audio file

Distortion Removes or adds distortion to an audio file as shown in Figure 7-25.

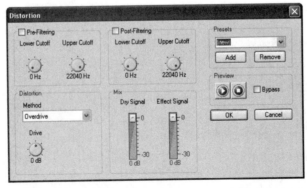

Figure 7-25: The Distortion dialog box lets you clean up distortion in your audio file

Multi-Tap Delay Creates multiple echoes of a sound, as shown in Figure 7-26.

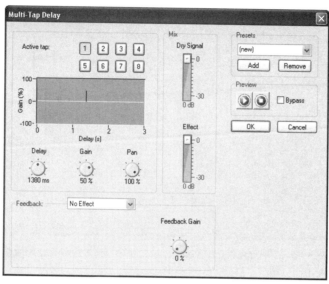

Figure 7-26: The Multi-Tap Delay dialog box lets you define different types of delays for your audio file

Modulation Changes the amplitude modulation and frequency modulation of an audio file, as shown in Figure 7-27.

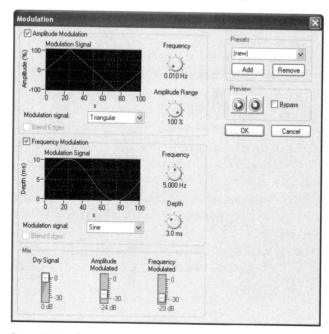

Figure 7-27: The Modulation dialog box lets you change the amplitude and frequency modulation

Re-analogue Makes a digital audio file sound like it was recorded from an old vinyl record or tape cassette, complete with tape hiss, crackles, and pops, as shown in Figure 7-28.

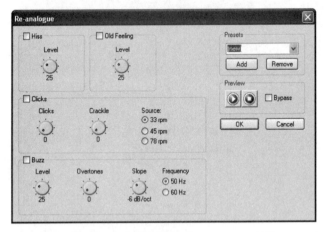

Figure 7-28: The Re-analogue dialog box gives you different options for mimicking tape hiss or vinyl record pops and crackles

Filtering Subsonic Frequencies

If you have a recording that sounds awful because the recording equipment wasn't calibrated correctly, you can use Nero's DC offset correction feature to remove subsonic frequencies. To use DC offset correction, follow these steps:

1. Follow the steps in the earlier "Running Nero Wave Editor" section to load the audio file you want to edit.

2. Click the part of the audio file that you want to correct. Nero displays a vertical line. You can adjust the position of this vertical line by pressing the left and right arrow keys.

3. Click and drag the mouse, or hold down the **SHIFT** key while pressing the left or right arrow key, to select part of your audio file. (If you want to select the entire audio file, press **CTRL+A**.)

4. Click the **Enhancement** menu and click **DC Offset Correction**. Nero displays the words "DC Offset Correction" above the part of the audio file you selected.

5. Click the **Audio** menu, and click **Play Selection** (or press the **SPACEBAR**) to hear how DC offset correction has modified the sound of the selected part of the audio file.

8

PLAYING AUDIO

Besides letting you burn your own CDs, Nero includes an audio player so you can listen to music on your computer. Not only can Nero play ordinary CDs, but it can also play a wide variety of audio file formats.

Listening to CDs and Audio Files

The Nero program for playing audio files is called NeroMix. To start the NeroMix program, follow these steps:

1. Start the StartSmart menu.
2. Click the **Audio** category.
3. Click **Play Audio**. The NeroMix window appears, as shown in Figure 8-1 on the next page.

In case you don't like the entire NeroMix program floating in the middle of your screen, you can display a miniature version by switching to Window-Shade mode. To toggle between WindowShade mode and full-size mode, click the **Toggle WindowShade Mode** button.

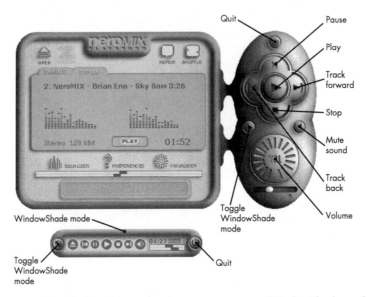

Figure 8-1: The NeroMix audio player can appear in WindowShade mode so it tucks out of the way, or in full-size mode so you can see everything easily

Playing an Entire Audio CD

With NeroMix, you can play all your favorite audio CDs. To play all the tracks stored on an audio CD, follow these steps:

1. Insert an audio CD into your CD or DVD drive. Windows displays a dialog box, asking what you want to do with your CD as shown in Figure 8-2. (If the Windows dialog box does not appear, follow the instructions listed in the next section, "Playing Select Tracks on Audio CDs.")

2. Click **Play Audio CD with NeroMix**. NeroMix starts playing your CD.

Figure 8-2: Whenever you insert a CD into your computer, Windows asks what you want to do with it

Playing Select Tracks on Audio CDs

Sometimes you may not want to play every possible track available, but just want to select a handful to hear. To select and play audio tracks with NeroMix, follow these steps:

1. Start up NeroMix.
2. Insert an audio CD into your CD or DVD drive.
3. Click the **Open** icon. An Open dialog box appears.
4. Click in the **Look in** list box and click the CD or DVD drive that contains your audio CD. The Open dialog box displays a list of tracks with generic names, such as Track 1 or Track 8.
5. Click the tracks that you want to play. To select multiple tracks, hold down the **CTRL** key and click each track you want to hear. If you want to select a range of tracks, click the first track you want to hear, hold down the **SHIFT** key, and click the last track that you want to hear. NeroMix highlights the first and last tracks and all those in between.
6. Click the **Open** button.
7. Click one or more of the following:

    > **Repeat**   Plays your selected tracks endlessly until you finally click **Stop**
    >
    > **Shuffle**   Randomly plays songs until they have all been played once
    >
    > **Track back**   Plays the previous track
    >
    > **Track forward**   Plays the next track
    >
    > **Mute sound**   Keeps playing an audio track without playing any sound

8. Click **Play**.

Playing Different Audio File Formats

Although most audio players can recognize the common MP3 file format, NeroMix can also recognize some of the more obscure audio file formats, including Ogg Vorbis and TwinVQ. To play one or more digital audio files, follow these steps:

1. Start NeroMix.
2. Click the **Open** icon. An Open dialog box appears.
3. Click in the **Look in** list box and click the folder that contains your digital audio files.
4. Click the files that you want to play. To select multiple tracks, hold down the **CTRL** key and click each track you want to hear. If you want to select a range of tracks, click the first track you want to hear, hold down the **SHIFT** key, and click the last track that you want to hear. NeroMix highlights the first and last tracks and all those in between.

5. Click the **Open** button.

6. Click one or more of the following:

> **Repeat**   Plays your selected tracks endlessly until you finally click **Stop**
>
> **Shuffle**   Randomly plays songs until they have all been played once
>
> **Track back**   Plays the previous track
>
> **Track forward**   Plays the next track
>
> **Mute sound**   Keeps playing an audio track without playing any sound

7. Click **Play**.

Changing Songs

If you like a particular song or part of a song, NeroMix can help you jump there. NeroMix offers three methods to jump to a particular song, as shown in Figures 8-1 and 8-3:

*   Click the **Playlist** tab and double-click the song you want to hear.

*   Click the **Track back** or **Track forward** buttons to hear the previous audio track or the next audio track.

*   Drag the **Track selection slider** right or left. As you drag the Track selection slider, NeroMix displays the currently selected track number and title.

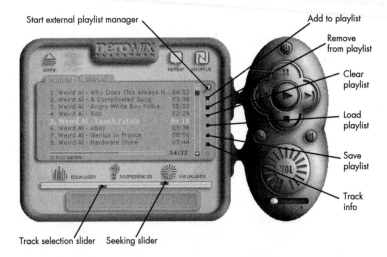

Figure 8-3: NeroMix offers three different ways to jump to an audio track that you want to hear

Once you start listening to your favorite song, you may want to skip back or ahead to a different part of the song. To hear a different part of the currently playing song, just drag the **Seeking slider** right or left, where the far left of the slider represents the beginning of the audio track and the far right represents the end of the audio track.

Repeating Songs

When you load an audio CD or a bunch of audio files, such as MP3 files, NeroMix displays a list of all the songs it will play. This list, called a playlist, shows you all the songs that NeroMix will play at least once before stopping. But NeroMix can play a single song or your entire playlist repeatedly if you want.

To play a single song repeatedly, follow these steps:

1. Click the audio track you want to play repeatedly.
2. Click the **Repeat** button. The Repeat button displays the number 1. At this point, NeroMix will do nothing but play your chosen song over and over again until you tell it to stop.

To play an entire playlist over and over again, follow these steps:

1. Click the **Repeat** button. The Repeat button displays the number 1.
2. Click the **Repeat** button again. The Repeat button now displays ALL. At this point, NeroMix will play all the songs in your playlist until you tell it to stop.

To stop repeating songs, click the **Repeat** button until it no longer displays the number 1 or the word ALL.

Creating and Using Playlists

The playlist always shows the order in which NeroMix will play your audio tracks, from first to last. (If you click the **Shuffle** button, NeroMix ignores the order of audio tracks in the playlist and plays audio tracks out of order.) To view the playlist, just click the **Playlist** tab.

Rearranging Audio Tracks in a Playlist

If you want to change the order in which your audio tracks play, you can rearrange them by clicking and dragging an audio track to a new location in the playlist and then releasing the mouse button. NeroMix will now play your audio tracks in your new order (unless you click the **Shuffle** button to make NeroMix play your audio tracks in a random order).

Adding Audio Tracks to a Playlist

If you have a collection of digital audio files stored on your computer, you can create different lists of favorite songs to match your mood, such as love songs or dance songs. Of course, you will probably want to keep adding songs to your playlists as you collect more music. Fortunately, NeroMix lets you add new audio tracks to your playlist at any time.

To add a song to a playlist, follow these steps:

1. Click the **Add to playlist** button, shown in Figure 8-3 on page 122. An Open dialog box appears.
2. Click the audio file that you want to add. If you hold down the CTRL key, you can click and select multiple audio files. If you hold down the SHIFT key, click one audio file and then click another audio file, NeroMix will select the first and last files and every file in between.
3. Click the **Open** button. NeroMix adds your chosen audio files to your playlist.

Removing Audio Tracks from a Playlist

If you've added a bunch of digital audio files to your playlist, you may have included one or two that you don't want to hear after all. Fortunately, NeroMix lets you remove audio tracks from your playlists.

NOTE *When you remove an audio track from a playlist, you aren't physically deleting the file from your computer.*

To remove an audio track from your playlist, click the track and then click the **Remove from playlist** button. NeroMix removes your chosen audio track.

If you want to remove all the audio tracks from your playlist, click the **Clear playlist** button instead. When a dialog box appears, click **Yes** to clear your entire playlist or **Cancel** if you've changed your mind.

Saving and Loading a Playlist

After taking the time to choose and arrange your favorite songs in different playlists, you can save them as playlist files. That way you can just open that one playlist file, and NeroMix will automatically play all the songs in the order you arranged them in your playlist.

To save a playlist, follow these steps:

1. Click the **Save Playlist** button. A Save Playlist dialog box appears.
2. Type a descriptive name for your playlist, and click **Save**. (You may want to change the drive and folder when you save your playlist.)

Once you've saved one or more playlists, you can load them again at any time by following these steps:

1. Click the **Load Playlist** button. A Load Playlist dialog box appears.
2. Click on the playlist you want to load and click **Open**. NeroMix displays all the songs stored in your chosen playlist.

Displaying and Changing Track Info

Every audio track contains both technical data (such as its file format) and descriptive data (such as the name of the song, the recording artist, and the album that the song came from). To view or edit the non-technical data about a particular audio track, follow these steps:

1. Click an audio track that you want to edit or view.
2. Click the **Track info** button. NeroMix displays a File Details dialog box, as shown in Figure 8-4.

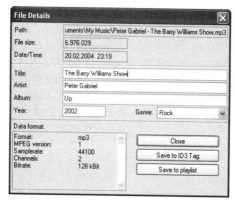

Figure 8-4: The File Details dialog box shows you the technical and descriptive details about your chosen audio file

3. (Optional.) Change the Title, Artist, Album, Year, or Genre data if you want, and then click the **Save to ID3 Tag** button to save the new track information.
4. Click **Close** if you skipped step 3, or click **Save to playlist** to save any changes you made in step 3.

Using the External Playlist Manager

In case you find it inconvenient to add, rearrange, and delete songs and save playlists within NeroMix, you can make all your changes to a playlist through NeroMix's external Playlist Manager window. To display this external Playlist Manager (shown in Figure 8-5 on the next page), just click the **Start external playlist manager** button.

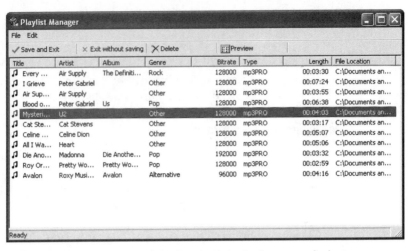

Figure 8-5: NeroMix's external Playlist Manager displays your playlist in a separate window for easier editing

Within this Playlist Manager, you can rearrange and delete audio tracks as well as save your altered playlist. To rearrange your playlist, just click and drag an audio track to a new location in the playlist and then release the mouse button. To delete an audio track, click it and then click the **Delete** button (or click the **Edit** menu and then click **Delete**).

After altering your playlist, click the **Save & Exit** button (to save your playlist) or the **Exit without saving** button (to discard any changes you made to your playlist).

Customizing NeroMix

Many people like to customize their audio players to reflect their own moods or personalities (or just to have something to do while sitting around at work). To modify the sound, NeroMix provides an equalizer that you can adjust. To modify the appearance of NeroMix, you can view visualizations, which are moving patterns that correspond to the music playing. For more fun, you can even change the entire appearance of NeroMix by giving it a new *skin*, so it looks like a floating coin or flaming disc.

Just remember that any changes you make to the visual appearance of NeroMix won't affect the way NeroMix plays your music. Changing the visual appearance of NeroMix is purely for your own amusement.

Adjusting Sound with the Equalizer

Most people are happy just popping an audio CD into their computer and listening to the music, but some people prefer tweaking the sound to make it as crisp and sharp as possible. To satisfy audio fanatics, NeroMix offers an equalizer so you can change various frequencies until it sounds best to you.

To display and adjust the equalizer, follow these steps:

1. Follow the steps in the previous "Playing Audio CDs" or "Playing Different Audio File Formats" sections to play a song.

2. Click the **Equaliser** icon. NeroMix displays the equalizer, as shown in Figure 8-6.

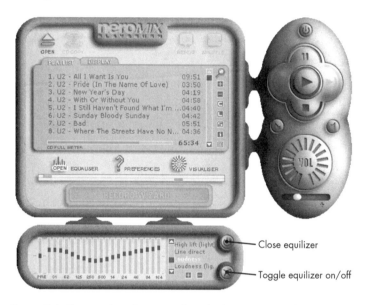

Close equilizer

Toggle equilizer on/off

Figure 8-6: The equalizer lets you adjust the frequencies until your music sounds exactly right to you

3. Click the **Toggle equalizer on/off** button so a check mark appears on the button.

4. Double-click a preset equalizer setting, such as **Cheap radio** or **Bass lift**, or adjust the individual vertical frequency sliders yourself.

5. Click the **Close equalizer** button to hide the equalizer from view.

Changing Skins

A *skin* is just a way to display NeroMix on your screen. In case you don't like the default appearance of NeroMix, you can pick a different skin and make NeroMix look like anything from a coin to a flaming disc to a handheld computer, as shown in Figure 8-7 on the next page. Such visual appearances are purely for your own amusement and won't affect the way NeroMix plays your audio tracks.

NOTE   *When you change the appearance of NeroMix with a different skin, the buttons for doing everything from playing a song to quitting NeroMix may suddenly be in completely different parts of the screen. Just move the mouse pointer over a button, and NeroMix will display a helpful hint that explains what that button does.*

Figure 8-7: NeroMix can use different skins to change its appearance drastically

To choose a different skin for NeroMix, follow these steps:

1. Click the **Preferences** icon. A Preferences dialog box appears.
2. Click **Skins** in the left side of the Preferences dialog box. A list of available skins is displayed, as shown in Figure 8-8.
3. Click a skin, such as **Flame** or **Coin**, and click **Close**. NeroMix appears in your chosen skin.

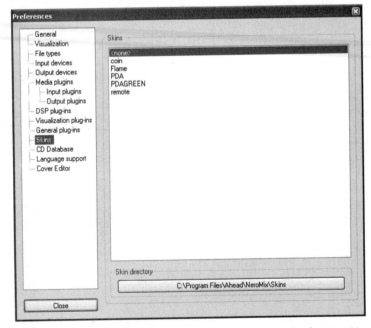

Figure 8-8: The Preferences dialog box lets you choose a skin for NeroMix

Staring at Visualizations

Most people like to listen to music while they're doing something else, but if you want to see something visually interesting on your computer while your music plays, NeroMix can display a visualization. Basically, a *visualization* is just a fancy, psychedelic display of colors and geometric shapes that appear to dance and pulse to the beat of the currently playing song. Visualizations don't affect the way NeroMix plays songs; it's just something interesting to watch.

To view a visualization, follow these steps:

1. Click the **Display** tab.
2. Click the **Visualiser** button. NeroMix displays visualizations that change colors and shapes based on your music.

To customize the way NeroMix displays visualizations, follow these steps:

1. Click the **Preferences** button. A Preferences dialog box appears.
2. Click **Visualization** in the left side of the Preferences dialog box to display the visualization settings, as shown in Figure 8-9.
3. Change any settings, and click **Close** to see the results.

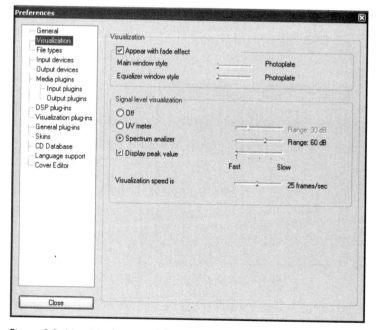

Figure 8-9: NeroMix lets you define visualization settings

Burning an Audio CD

If you're listening to an audio CD or a list of digital audio files that you like, NeroMix gives you the option of burning a copy of the currently displayed playlist to a disc. To burn an audio CD with NeroMix, follow these steps:

1. Click the **Stop** button. NeroMix can't play music and burn a CD at the same time. The **Record Wizard** button appears, as shown in Figure 8-10.

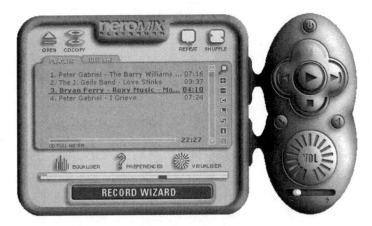

Figure 8-10: When you stop playing music, NeroMix gives you the option of burning your playlist to an audio CD

2. Click the **Record Wizard** button. A Wizard dialog box appears, as shown in Figure 8-11.

Figure 8-11: The Wizard dialog box lets you tell NeroMix what you want to do

3. Click in the list box at the top of the Wizard dialog box, and select **Record an Audio CD**.

4. Click **Next**. The Wizard dialog box now asks which rewritable CD or DVD drive to use, as shown in Figure 8-12.

Figure 8-12: The Wizard dialog box next asks which rewritable CD or DVD drive to use

5. Click in the list box, and choose the rewritable CD or DVD drive to use.

6. Click the **Options** button to display the Audio CD Recording Options dialog box, as shown in Figure 8-13.

Figure 8-13: The Audio CD Recording Options dialog box lets you specify whether to pause between each track or to cross-fade each track

7. Click the options you want, and click **OK** when you're finished.

8. Click **Next**. The Wizard dialog box lets you specify whether you want to test, simulate, or burn your audio CD. (If you click both the **Simulation** and **Burn** check boxes, NeroMix will first simulate burning an audio CD, and if the simulation succeeds, it will go ahead and burn the actual CD.)

9. Insert a blank CD in the rewritable CD or DVD drive that you chose in step 5.

10. Click **Finish**.

Converting Audio File Formats

Besides playing digital audio files, NeroMix can also convert digital audio files from one file format to another or "rip" audio tracks from an audio CD and store them in another digital file format.

To convert an audio track or file into another digital audio file format with NeroMix, follow these steps:

1. Click the **Stop** button. NeroMix can't play music and convert files at the same time. The Record Wizard button appears in red (see Figure 8-10 on page 130).

2. Click the **Record Wizard** button. A Wizard dialog box appears (see Figure 8-11 on page 130).

3. Click in the list box at the top of the Wizard dialog box, and select a file format option, such as **Create 'Windows Media Audio' audio files**.

4. Click the **Options** button. The Wizard dialog box displays a list of recording options for your digital audio files. (Depending on which file format you chose, the dialog box that appears may look different than the one shown in Figure 8-14.)

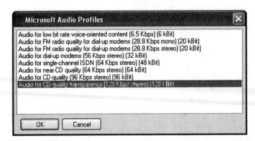

Figure 8-14: The Options button displays a dialog box so you can define the sound quality of your digital audio file

5. Click **OK** and then click **Next**. Another Wizard dialog box appears, asking you to choose your audio source.

6. Click in the list box at the top of the Wizard dialog box, and choose **Use tracks from my playlist**.

7. (Optional.) Click in the **Record the complete playlist** check box to clear it if you don't want to convert all the audio tracks displayed in your playlist. Click **Next**. NeroMix displays a dialog box to let you select the audio tracks you want to convert. Click the audio tracks you want to convert.

8. Click **Finish**. NeroMix converts all your chosen digital audio files to the file format you chose in step 3. When NeroMix is finished converting your digital audio files, it stores them in the MyMusic folder inside the Ahead folder on your hard disk.

9

PLAYING VIDEO

Nero includes a video player that lets you watch full-length DVD movies and video files on your computer. Nero can also capture still images from your movies so you can paste them into a graphics program and manipulate them later.

Playing DVDs and Video Files

The Nero program for playing video files is called Nero ShowTime. To start the Nero ShowTime program, follow these steps:

1. Start the StartSmart menu.
2. Click the **Photo and Video** category.
3. Click **Play Video**. The Nero ShowTime window appears.

Nero ShowTime actually consists of two parts: the viewing screen and the control panel. You can move both parts separately from one another and resize the viewing screen to fill up more or less of your computer screen.

Playing DVDs

With Nero ShowTime, you can play DVDs of your favorite movies. To play a DVD, follow these steps:

1. Start Nero ShowTime.
2. Insert a DVD into your DVD drive.
3. Click the **Select source** button. A pop-up menu appears.
4. Click the DVD drive that contains your DVD. Nero ShowTime starts playing your DVD.

Playing Digital Video Files

Nero ShowTime can play a wide variety of video files stored in different file formats, such as Windows Media or MPEG files. To play a video file, follow these steps:

1. Start Nero ShowTime.
2. Click the **Select source** button. A pop-up menu appears.
3. Click **Media Files** on the pop-up menu. An Open dialog box appears.
4. Click the file that you want to play. You may need to click in the **Look in** list box to change the drive.
5. Click the **Open** button. Nero ShowTime starts to play your chosen video file.

Controls for Watching a Video File or DVD

Whether you're watching a video file or a DVD, you may want to pause the video, expand or shrink the viewing screen, or capture a frame. Nero ShowTime provides two ways to control your video as you're watching it: by clicking on controls, as shown in Figure 9-1, or by pressing keys on the keyboard.

If you choose to display the viewing window in full-screen mode, the controls temporarily disappear. You can still control Nero ShowTime by using the keyboard commands listed in Table 9-1. Or you can click in the viewing area or move the mouse to the very top of the window to make the controls appear once more.

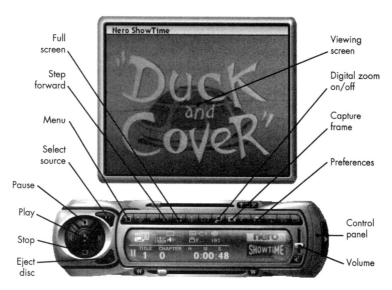

Figure 9-1: Nero ShowTime provides different options for controlling your movie while you're watching it

Table 9-1: Keyboard Commands for Controlling a Video

Command	What it does	Keyboard command
Pause	Temporarily freezes your movie	SPACEBAR
Stop	Stops playing your movie	S
Play	Plays your movie after the **Pause** or **Stop** command has stopped it	ENTER
Previous chapter	Rewinds to the previous chapter of your movie (many DVD movies are divided into parts called chapters, which lets you jump to a scene in the middle of a movie without having to scroll through the entire movie from the beginning)	P
Next chapter	Fast-forwards to the next chapter of your movie	N
Go to bookmark	Jumps to a previously defined bookmark	G
Menu	Displays the root menu of the DVD (may not do anything when playing a digital video file)	L
Step forward	Advances one frame forward	T
Full screen	Expands or shrinks the viewing window to fill the entire computer screen (double-clicking the viewing window also toggles between full-screen and normal-screen modes)	Z

Table 9-1: Keyboard Commands for Controlling a Video

Command	What it does	Keyboard command
Digital zoom on/off	Allows you to examine a rectangular part of your movie	D
Capture frame	Captures a frame from your video	C
Preferences	Displays the Preferences dialog box for customizing the way Nero ShowTime works	CTRL+C
Repeat	Keeps playing your movie over and over until you click the **Stop** button	CTRL+R
Add bookmark	Lets you bookmark a specific frame that you can jump to later using the **Go to bookmark** command	M
Volume	Raises or lowers the volume	Up arrow (raises volume), down arrow (lowers volume). Scrolling the mouse wheel raises or lowers the volume.
Forward	Fast-forwards your video	F
Rewind	Rewinds your video	B

Using Digital Zoom

While viewing a video, you may suddenly see part of an image that you'd like to see in greater detail, such as somebody's face. Rather than squint and stare at the tiny detail, Nero ShowTime lets you zoom in and see that part of the image as a close-up.

To zoom in to part of an image, follow these steps:

1. Click the **Pause** button when you see the frame that displays the detail that you want to view.

2. Click the **Digital zoom on/off** button (or press the **D** key). The mouse pointer turns into a crosshair icon.

3. Move the mouse pointer to one corner of the image that you want to blow up.

4. Click and drag the mouse to draw a rectangle over the image that you want to see.

5. Release the mouse button. Nero ShowTime displays your selected area as a close-up.

Capturing a Frame

Nero ShowTime can capture a frame from your favorite movie so you can paste it into a graphics program, save it as a separate file, or make it part of your desktop wallpaper. To tell Nero ShowTime how to save a captured frame, follow these steps:

1. Click the **Preferences** button (or press CTRL+C). The Preferences dialog box appears. The left panel of the Preferences dialog box displays a list of different settings you can change, such as Toolbar setting or Audio. The right panel of the Preferences dialog box displays the different ways you can change the setting you chose in the left panel.

2. In the left panel of the Preferences dialog box, click the plus sign (+) to the left of **General**. The Preferences dialog box displays a list of setting options.

3. Click **Capture Frame** in the left panel. The Preferences dialog box displays the Capture Frame settings in the right panel, as shown in Figure 9-2.

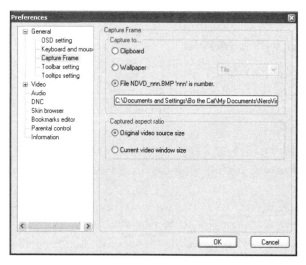

Figure 9-2: The Preferences dialog box lets you define how to save a captured frame from a movie

4. Click one of the following radio buttons in the **Capture to** group:

    Clipboard   Pastes your captured frame on the Windows Clipboard so you can paste it into another program

    Wallpaper   Turns your captured frame into the Windows desktop wallpaper

    File   Saves your captured frame as a bitmap graphics file in the drive and folder you specify

5. Click one of the following radio buttons in the **Captured Aspect Ratio** group:

> **Original video source size**   Captures the frame from the video regardless of the current size of the viewing window
>
> **Current video window size**   Captures the frame based on the current size of the viewing window

6. Click **OK.**

Once you've defined your preferences for capturing a frame, you can capture a frame from a video by following these steps:

1. Click the **Pause** button to freeze the frame that you want to capture. (It's actually possible to capture a frame without pausing, but pausing lets you see the exact frame you're going to capture.)
2. (Optional.) Follow the steps in the "Using Digital Zoom" section if you want to capture a close-up of an image in a frame.
3. Click the **Capture frame** button (or press the **C** key). Nero ShowTime captures your chosen frame.

Navigating Through a Movie

While you're watching a movie, you may be tempted to replay a scene or skip over a boring part of the movie. Fortunately, Nero ShowTime provides several different controls to rewind or forward your movie, as shown in Figure 9-3:

> **Seek slider**   Lets you rewind or fast forward your movie.
>
> **Forward and Rewind**   Rewinds or forwards your movie at different speeds.
>
> **Chapter slider**   Lets you rewind or forward to a different chapter in your movie. (Chapters are usually only found on commercial DVDs.)
>
> **Bookmarks**   Lets you mark a scene and jump back to it at a later time.

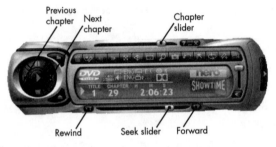

Figure 9-3: Nero ShowTime provides different ways to view different parts of your movie

Using the Seek Slider and the Forward and Rewind Buttons

The Seek slider gives you manual control in rewinding or fast-forwarding your movie. The disadvantage is that it can be clumsy to use, because you won't know how far back or forward to drag the slider to view the part of the movie that you want to see. To use the Seek slider, click the **Seek slider** and drag it to the left or right.

The Rewind and Forward buttons give you the option to rewind or fast-forward your movie at different speeds. As the movie rewinds or fast-forwards, you can watch the scenes flash by and click the **Play** button when you see the part of the movie you want to watch.

To use the Rewind or Forward buttons, follow these steps:

1. Click the **Rewind** button (or press the **B** key) or the **Forward** button (or press the **F** key). A pop-up menu appears, as shown in Figure 9-4.

Figure 9-4: The Rewind and Forward buttons display a pop-up menu for you to choose the speed for rewinding or fast-forwarding your movie

2. Click a speed for rewinding or forwarding your movie. Nero starts rewinding or forwarding your movie at your chosen speed.
3. Click the **Play** button when you see the part of the movie you want to watch.

Using the Chapter Slider

Most commercial DVDs divide full-length movies into multiple chapters, which you can view without having to see any other parts of the movie. To jump through the different chapters of a movie, Nero ShowTime provides two options:

• Use the Chapter slider
• Use the Next chapter and Previous chapter buttons

The Chapter slider lets you jump to a different chapter quickly. To use the Chapter slider, follow these steps:

1. Click the **Chapter slider** and drag the mouse left or right. As you drag the Chapter slider, a tooltip appears, displaying the current chapter number that Nero ShowTime will display when you release the mouse button.

2. Release the mouse button when you see the chapter number that you want to watch.

If you know you want to view the previous or next chapter, you may find the Previous chapter and Next chapter buttons more convenient to use:

1. Click the **Previous chapter** button (or press the **P** key) or the **Next chapter** button (or press the **N** key). Nero ShowTime displays the previous or next chapter.

2. Repeat step 1 until you see the chapter you want to watch.

Using Bookmarks

If you want to jump to a particular point within a chapter, or if you're watching a video that isn't divided into chapters, you can use a bookmark to mark a particular frame that you can jump back to at a later time.

NOTE *Nero stores bookmarks on your hard disk, usually in the C:\Documents and Settings\ User Name\Application Data\Ahead folder unless you specify a different location. Because Nero stores bookmarks on your hard disk, they won't travel with your DVD if you play them in another computer.*

Creating a Bookmark

To create a bookmark, follow these steps:

1. (Optional.) Click the **Pause** button. (You can add a bookmark without pausing your movie, but pausing lets you see the exact frame where you're setting a bookmark.)

2. Click the **Add a bookmark** button (or press the **M** key).

Jumping to a Bookmark

Nero ShowTime provides two ways to jump to a bookmark:

- Jumping to the first bookmark and sequentially displaying each subsequent bookmark you created

- Jumping straight to a particular bookmark

Jumping to the first bookmark is faster, but if you created many bookmarks, having to scroll through them one by one from the beginning can be time-consuming and annoying. Jumping straight to a bookmark may be more convenient, but Nero ShowTime forces you to open a dialog box first and then click the bookmark you want, so this method is a bit clumsier.

To jump from one bookmark to the next, follow these steps:

1. Click the **Go to bookmark** button (or press the **G** key). Nero ShowTime jumps to the first bookmark you created.

2. Repeat step 1 to step through all your bookmarks one by one until you find the bookmarked scene you want to watch.

To jump to a specific bookmark right away, follow these steps:

1. Click the **Preferences** button (or press **CTRL+C**). The Preferences dialog box appears.

2. Click **Bookmarks editor** in the left pane of the Preferences dialog box, as shown in Figure 9-5.

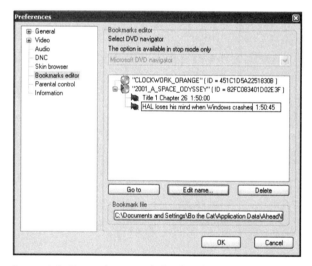

Figure 9-5: The Preferences dialog box lets you edit, rename, and jump to a specific bookmark

3. Click the bookmark that you want to jump to, and click the **Go to** button.

Editing a Bookmark

When you create a bookmark, Nero ShowTime gives it a generic name, such as "Title 1 Chapter 26." Because this isn't likely to tell you anything about the scene that you bookmarked, you may want to type a more descriptive name for your bookmark.

To edit a bookmark's name, follow these steps:

1. Click the **Preferences** button (or press CTRL+C). The Preferences dialog box appears.
2. Click **Bookmarks editor** in the left pane of the Preferences dialog box (see Figure 9-5 on the previous page).
3. Click the bookmark that you want to change, and click the **Edit name** button. Nero ShowTime highlights your chosen bookmark's name.
4. Type a new name, or press the BACKSPACE or **left** or **right arrow** keys to edit your bookmark's name.
5. Click **OK** when you're finished.

Deleting a Bookmark

You may eventually want to delete some of your bookmarks. To delete a bookmark, follow these steps:

1. Click the **Preferences** button (or press CTRL+C). The Preferences dialog box appears.
2. Click **Bookmarks editor** in the left pane of the Preferences dialog box (see Figure 9-5 on the previous page).
3. Click the bookmark that you want to delete, and click the **Delete** button. Nero ShowTime deletes your chosen bookmark.
4. Click **OK** when you're finished.

10

RECORDING AUDIO FROM LPs AND TAPES

Although most people listen to audio CDs or digital audio files, many people still have music trapped on old tape cassettes and vinyl records (affectionately known as LPs, which stands for *Long Playing*). While many people simply bought CD versions of their favorite albums, many records were never converted to CD, so people may still have rare vinyl records that will never be available as CDs.

Fortunately, you can still preserve the music in your vinyl record or tape cassette collection by converting them to CDs yourself. Once you convert the music from your records or tapes to digital audio files on your computer, you can burn them to a CD to preserve them forever (or until you lose the CD) or just play them on your computer or portable music player.

Connecting Your Stereo to Your Computer

Before you can transfer the music from your records and tapes to your computer, you need to buy an audio cable. One end of this cable needs to plug into the digital input port of your sound card, and the other end needs to plug into your stereo — the headphones jack or audio out plugs.

What you're doing is capturing the sound from your records or tapes and recording them on your computer. In technical terms, you're taking an analog signal and converting it into a digital one, which means that the sound quality may degrade a bit during the conversion.

Fortunately, the Nero SoundTrax program can modify the sound quality to eliminate any tape hiss, vinyl record pops, and other forms of noise degradation normally associated with vinyl and tape. Once you store your music on your computer, you can make it sound as crisp and clean as if it had been stored on an audio CD in the first place.

NOTE   *If the music industry ever comes up with a copy-protected audio CD that Nero can't copy correctly, you can just play the copy-protected audio CD on a stereo that's connected to your computer and capture the audio tracks as if you were recording them from a tape or record.*

Converting LPs and Tapes

After you have physically connected your stereo to your computer's sound card, you are ready to start the conversion process. Follow these steps:

1. Start the StartSmart menu.
2. Click the **Standard Mode** button so the words "Expert Mode" appear in the StartSmart menu.
3. Click the **Audio** category.
4. Click **Convert Tape to CD** or **Convert LP to CD**, depending on your music source. The Nero SoundTrax window appears and displays a Tape to CD Wizard (or LP to CD Wizard) dialog box, as shown in Figure 10-1.
5. Click in the **Audio input line** list box and choose an input, such as **Auxiliary**.
6. Play your vinyl record or tape cassette, and watch the Level Meters.
7. Adjust the **Recording Volume** slider. To capture the sound at the best volume level, adjust the Recording Volume slider until both Level Meters peak in the yellow part of the Level Meter. If the Recording Volume is too high, the Level Meter will display red and any music you capture may sound garbled or distorted. If the Recording Volume is too low, you'll only see green and any music that you capture may sound faint or muffled.
8. Click the **Change Target File** button. A Save As dialog box appears.

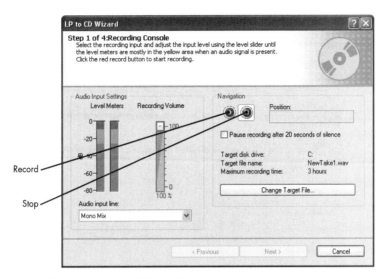

Figure 10-1: Step 1 of the Wizard lets you adjust the recording level of the sound coming from your tape or record

9. Type a name for the audio file, and select the drive and folder where you want to store it. You can also click in the **Save as type** list box to define the file format for your audio file.

10. Click the **Pause recording after 20 seconds of silence** check box. By checking this option, you can keep Nero from recording silence after your tape or record has finished playing.

11. Start your tape or record from the beginning again, and click the **Record** button.

12. Click **Next** when your tape cassette or vinyl record is done playing. Nero displays a second Wizard dialog box, as shown in Figure 10-2 on the next page. This second Wizard dialog box lets you tell Nero how to identify the end of an audio track.

13. Click on the **Silence Threshold** dial and drag it left or right to define the amount of noise that defines the end of an audio track. If you set this threshold too high, Nero may incorrectly break a quiet audio track in half.

14. Click in the **Minimum Duration of Pause** box and type a value or click the up and down arrows to define the minimum length of a pause that identifies the end of a track. If you set too long a time, Nero could incorrectly merge two audio tracks together.

15. Click in the **Minimum Duration of Track** box and type a value or click on the up and down arrows to define the minimum length of a track. If you set this value too small, Nero might incorrectly divide an audio track into several parts.

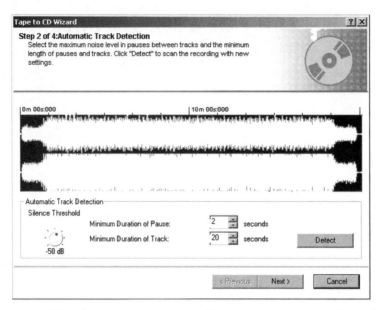

Figure 10-2: After you've captured sound from your tape or record, you can tell Nero SoundTrax how to find individual audio tracks

16. Click **Next**. Nero displays a third Wizard dialog box, as shown in Figure 10-3. This third Wizard dialog box helps reduce tape hiss or pops and crackles on records.

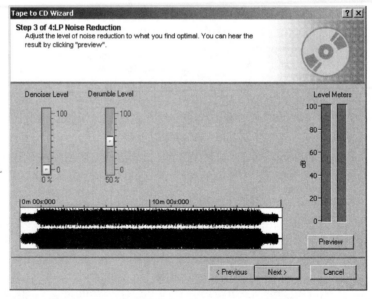

Figure 10-3: The third Wizard dialog box can reduce the noise of your recordings

17. Click the **Preview** button to hear your audio track.

18. Click on and drag the **Denoiser Level** and the **Derumble Level** sliders up or down until you like the sound of your audio track.

19. Click **Next**. Nero displays a fourth Wizard dialog box, as shown in Figure 10-4. This fourth Wizard dialog box lets you define how to burn your audio tracks to a CD.

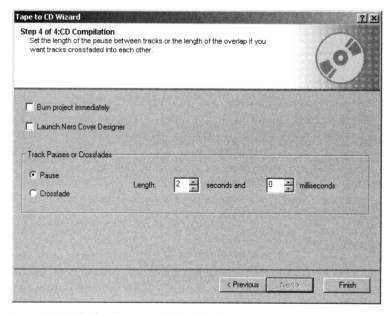

Figure 10-4: The fourth Wizard dialog box lets you tell Nero how long to pause between audio tracks

20. Click the **Pause** or **Crossfade** radio button, and click in the **Length** options to specify the length of your pauses or the extent of your crossfades.

21. (Optional.) Click the **Burn project immediately** check box if you want to burn your audio tracks to a CD right away.

22. Click **Finish**. At this point, you can copy or rename your saved audio tracks to another folder or drive, or you can burn them to a CD at a later date. If you clicked the Burn project immediately check box in step 21, follow steps 23–25 when Nero displays the dialog box shown in Figure 10-5 on the next page.

23. Click in the **Device** list box and click on the rewritable CD or DVD drive that you want to use.

24. Insert a blank CD-R or CD+RW disc in the drive you selected in step 23.

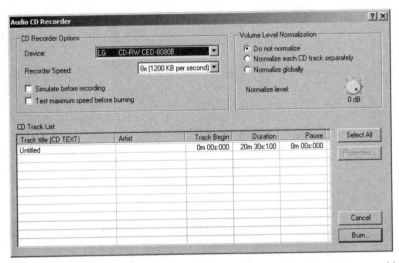

Figure 10-5: The Audio CD Recorder dialog box lets you specify which rewritable CD or DVD drive to use and how long to pause between tracks

25. Click on one of the following radio buttons within the **Volume Level Normalization** group:

> **Do not normalize**   Burns all your audio tracks at whatever volume level they may have been recorded at.

> **Normalize each CD track separately**   Lets you adjust the volume level of each audio track. This can be time-consuming, but it gives you maximum control over the way each audio track sounds.

> **Normalize globally**   Adjusts the volume of all your audio tracks to the same volume level.

26. Click in the **Recorder Speed** list box and choose a speed, such as **8x**. (You may also want to click the **Test maximum speed before burning** check box to make sure Nero can successfully burn your CD at the recording speed you chose.)

27. Click in the **Simulate before recording** check box if you want to make sure Nero can successfully burn your CD before actually starting to burn it.

28. Click in the **CD Track List** table to edit the track title or artist.

29. Click **Burn**. Nero burns your CD.

11

CAPTURING AND EDITING VIDEO

If you have old family movies stored on video cassettes or the latest footage of your birthday party stored on your digital video camera, you can use Nero to transfer your movies to DVDs. Once you've captured your movies to your hard disk, Nero can convert them to a variety of file formats so you can share your creations with your friends, family, and coworkers so they can see what you really look like in front of a video camera.

Transferring Movies to Nero

You have two ways of transferring your movies to Nero, depending on where they are stored.

- **Digital video cameras**   If you have a digital video camera, you just need to connect a FireWire (also known as IEEE 1394 and iLink) cable from your digital video camera to a FireWire port on your computer.

- **Video cassettes**   If your movies are trapped on video cassettes, you'll have to connect your VCR or video camera to a special device that converts your analog video signal to digital. First, you plug your VCR or video camera into the converter. Then you connect the converter to your computer through a FireWire or USB port. Companies that sell analog-to-digital converters include Canopus (www.canopus.com), Miglia (www.miglia.com), and Pinnacle Systems (www.pinnaclesys.com).

Once you have the proper hardware necessary to transfer your movies from a video camera or VCR to your computer (a FireWire cable or analog-to-digital video converter), you can store your movies on your hard disk by following these steps:

1. Start the StartSmart menu.

2. Click the **Photo and Video** category.

3. Connect your digital video camera or analog-to-digital converter to your computer's FireWire or USB port.

4. Click **Capture Video**. The NeroVision Express window appears, as shown in Figure 11-1.

Figure 11-1: The NeroVision Express window lets you view and record the part of your videotape that you want to keep

5. Click the **More** button. NeroVision Express displays additional options, as shown in Figure 11-2.

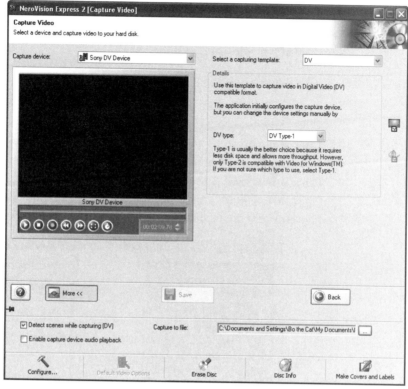

Figure 11-2: The More button displays the drive and folder where Nero will store your captured video

6. Click the **Capture to File** button. A Choose a Location for Your Captured Files dialog box appears.

7. Click in the **Saved in** list box, and choose a drive or folder where you want to store your captured videos. Click **Save**.

8. Click **Play** to view your video.

9. Click **Record** when you want to start recording.

10. Click **Stop** when you want to stop recording your video.

11. Click **Next**. The NeroVision Express window appears.

12. Click **Exit**. Nero stores your captured video in the folder you chose in step 6. You can use the Nero ShowTime program to view the video you captured on your hard disk.

Editing Digital Video Files

Once you've captured a video to your hard disk, you may want to take some time to trim the beginning or end to get rid of any excess video footage. In addition, you may want to divide your video into parts so you can quickly jump to a different part of your video without having to scroll through the whole video just to find a particular scene.

Trimming Video

Trimming a video lets you start and end a video at the precise moments you want. To trim a video, follow these steps:

1. Start the StartSmart menu.
2. Click the **Standard Mode** button to display the expert mode options.
3. Click the **Photo and Video** category.
4. Click **Make Movie**. The NeroVision Express window appears.
5. Click the **Browse for Media** button. A pop-up menu appears.
6. Click **Browse and Add to Project**. An Open dialog box appears.
7. Click the video file you want to trim, and click **Open**. Nero displays your chosen video file in the Storyboard view, as shown in Figure 11-3.

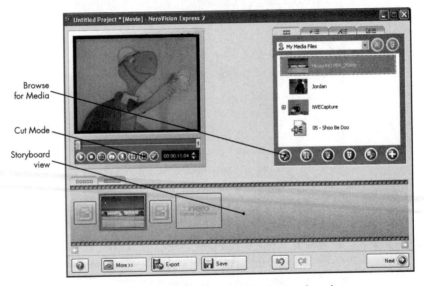

Browse for Media

Cut Mode

Storyboard view

Figure 11-3: You can trim a video file after you store it in the Storyboard view

8. Click the **Cut Mode** button. Nero displays a dialog box to let you know you can now trim your video.
9. Click **OK**. Nero displays the **Start of Cut Range** and **End of Cut Range** sliders, as shown in Figure 11-4.
10. Drag the **Start of Cut Range** slider until you see the first frame in the range that you want to trim from your video file.
11. Drag the **End of Cut Range** slider until you see the last frame in the range that you want to trim from your video file.
12. Click the **Cut Mode** button. Nero displays a dialog box, asking whether you really want to cut the part of the video you selected in steps 10 and 11.
13. Click **Yes**. Nero cuts out your selected part of the video file.

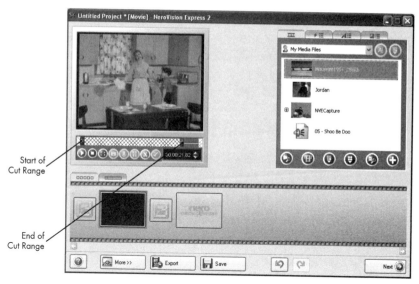

Start of
Cut Range

End of
Cut Range

Figure 11-4: The Cut Range sliders let you define what parts of a video to keep

NOTE *Once you've trimmed your video, you need to save your changes by clicking the **Save** or **Export** button.*

Dividing a Video

If you have a long movie, you may want to break it into smaller sections so you can put transitions in between each section or rearrange the order that a video plays in.

To divide a video into parts, follow these steps:

1. Start the StartSmart menu.
2. Click the **Standard Mode** button to display the expert mode options.
3. Click the **Photo and Video** category.
4. Click **Make Movie**. The NeroVision Express window appears.
5. Click the **Browse for Media** button. A pop-up menu appears.
6. Click **Browse and Add to Project**. An Open dialog box appears.
7. Click the video file you want to edit, and click **Open**. Nero displays your chosen video file in the Storyboard view.
8. Drag the **Position Marker** (which normally appears just to the right of the **Start of Cut Range** slider) to the left or right. Nero displays the currently selected frame, as shown in Figure 11-5 on the next page.
9. Click the **Split Item** button when you see the frame where you want to divide your video. Nero displays the cut portion of your video in a separate area of the Storyboard view.

NOTE *Once you've split your video, you need to save your changes by clicking the **Save** or **Export** button.*

Position Marker

Split Item

Figure 11-5: Nero can divide a large video into smaller parts

Splitting a Video Automatically

If the idea of dividing a video manually sounds like too much trouble, you can let Nero split your video up into different scenes automatically. The way Nero splits up your video depends on two settings: Sensitivity and Minimum Scene Length.

The Sensitivity defines how Nero decides to divide a video into two separate scenes based on changes from one frame to the next. The higher the Sensitivity, the more likely Nero will split a video the moment one frame changes from the previous frame. The lower the Sensitivity, the more drastic changes must be within two adjoining frames before Nero will split the video.

Minimum Scene Length defines how long part of a video must be before Nero will consider it to be a separate scene. The higher the scene length setting, the longer Nero waits before splitting a video. You may need to adjust both the Sensitivity and Minimum Scene Length settings to make Nero split your video accurately.

To split a video automatically, follow these steps:

1. Click on a video file that appears in the Display Media window.
2. Click the **Detect Scenes** button. A Scene Detection dialog box appears as shown in Figure 11-6.
3. Drag the **Sensitivity** slider.
4. Drag the **Minimum Scene Length** slider.

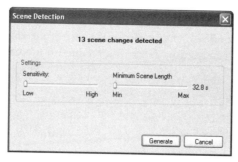

Figure 11-6: The Scene Detection dialog box lets you adjust the sensitivity and minimum scene length settings for automatically splitting a video

5. Click **Generate**. Nero splits your video and displays all the split scenes in the Display Media window as shown in Figure 11-7. You may need to click a plus (+) button that appears to the left of your original video to view all the split scenes.

Figure 11-7: Nero displays all the scenes that it split from your original video

Saving a Video

Once you've trimmed or split up your video, you can save it as part of a NeroVision project or as a separate, exported video file. If you save your edited video as a NeroVision project, you can add transitions, video effects, text, and audio to create a full-fledged multimedia presentation. If you export your edited video file, you'll just create a video file by itself with no transitions or visual effects.

Creating a NeroVision Project

A NeroVision project allows you to add audio and visual transitions to video so you can create a presentation. NeroVision can also include the following:

- **Visual effects** Alters the way your video appears, such as by distorting or coloring it
- **Text effects** Allows you to add text that can appear over your video
- **Transitions** Connects separate video scenes with visual effects, such as wipes or fades

Applying Visual Effects to Your Video

If your video looks too boring, you can spice up its appearance by applying different visual effects. To add visual effects to your video, follow these steps:

1. Start the StartSmart menu.
2. Click the **Standard Mode** button to display the expert mode options.
3. Click the **Photo and Video** category.
4. Click **Make Movie**. The NeroVision Express window appears and displays the last project you worked on.
5. (Optional.) Click **Next** if you want to load a new project, and then click the **Open Saved Project or Disc Image** button. When an Open dialog box appears, click the project you want to edit, and click **Open**. Nero displays your chosen project.
6. Click the **Display Video Effects** tab.
7. Click the **Subgroup** list box and choose a subgroup, such as **Filters** or **Color Filter**. Nero displays a list of visual effects you can apply to your video, as shown in Figure 11-8.

Figure 11-8: The Display Video Effects tab provides different ways to alter the appearance of your video

8. Click a visual effect, such as **Distortion – Water**, and click **Add to Project**. Nero adds your chosen effect to the Effects row in the Timeline view.

9. (Optional.) Move the mouse pointer over the visual effect until the mouse cursor turns into a four-way arrow. Click the left mouse button, and drag the mouse left or right to move the visual effect to a new position in your video.

10. (Optional.) Move the mouse pointer over the left or right edge of the visual effect until the mouse pointer turns into a two-way arrow. Click the left mouse button, and drag the mouse to expand or shrink the duration of your visual effect.

11. Click **Play**. As the position marker moves across your visual effect, Nero shows how that visual effect alters the appearance of your video, as shown in Figure 11-9.

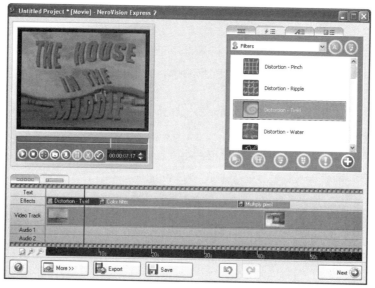

Figure 11-9: A visual effect can alter the appearance of your video when it plays

Adding Text Effects to Your Video

To emphasize certain parts of your video, you may want to include text effects. A text effect simply displays text while your video plays. The text can fade in and out, or twirl around the screen before stopping in the center.

To add text effects to your video, follow these steps:

1. Start the StartSmart menu.

2. Click the **Standard Mode** button to display the expert mode options.

3. Click the **Photo and Video** category.

4. Click **Make Movie**. The NeroVision Express window appears and displays the last project you worked on.

5. (Optional.) Click **Next** if you want to load a new project, and then click **Open Saved Project or Disc Image**. When an Open dialog box appears, click the project you want to edit, and click **Open**. Nero displays your chosen project.

6. Click the **Display Text Effects** tab. Nero displays a list of various visual effects you can apply to your text, as shown in Figure 11-10.

Figure 11-10: The Display Text Effects tab lets you customize the way text appears on the screen

7. Click a text effect, such as **Fade In/Out**, and click **Add to Project**. Nero adds your chosen effect to the Text row in the Timeline view and displays a Properties dialog box so you can customize the appearance of your text, as shown in Figure 11-11.

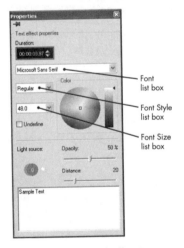

Figure 11-11: The text effect Properties dialog box lets you type in text and choose how it appears

8. Click the up and down arrows in the **Duration** list box to define the length of time you want your text to appear in your video. (You can also expand or shrink the length of time for your text effect. To do so, move the mouse along the left or right edge of the text effect in the Timeline view until the mouse pointer turns into a two-way arrow. Click the left mouse button and drag the mouse left or right.)

9. Click in the **Font** list box, and click on a font to use for your text.

10. Click in the **Font Style** list box, and click on a style, such as **Regular** or **Italic**.

11. Click in the **Font Size** list box, and click on a size for your text, such as **48**.

12. Click the color wheel to choose a color for your text.

13. Drag the **Opacity** and **Distance** sliders in the **Light source** group to define how your text appears.

14. Click in the text box at the bottom of the dialog box, and type the text that you want to appear over your video.

15. Click the close box of the Properties dialog box.

16. Click **Play**. As the position marker moves across your text effect, Nero shows your text over your video.

Making Transitions Within Your Video

If you break your video into several parts (as explained in the previous "Dividing a Video" section), you can add transitions between the scenes. Such transitions allow you to fade the last frame of the previous scene out and fade in the first frame of the next scene. You can also add transitions to the start or end of your video so your video dissolves into view and fades away at the end.

To add transitions to your video, follow these steps:

1. Start the StartSmart menu.

2. Click the **Standard Mode** button to display the expert mode options.

3. Click the **Photo and Video** category.

4. Click **Make Movie**. The NeroVision Express window appears and displays the last project you worked on.

5. (Optional.) Click **Next** if you want to load a new project, and then click **Open Saved Project or Disc Image**. When an Open dialog box appears, click the project you want to edit, and click **Open**. Nero displays your chosen project.

6. Click the **Storyboard** tab. Nero displays the Storyboard view.

7. Click the **Display Transitions** tab. Nero displays a list of transitions to choose from, as shown in Figure 11-12 on the next page.

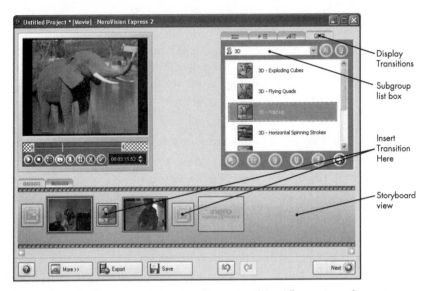

Figure 11-12: The Display Transitions tab shows you all the different types of transitions you can have between scenes or at the start or end of a video

8. Click in the **Subgroup** list box, and choose a group of transitions, such as **Fades** or **Wipes**.

9. Move the mouse over a transition, and click and drag the transition to an **Insert Transition Here** box where you want the transition to appear, such as between two scenes.

10. Click **Play** to see how your transition will look.

Removing Transitions and Effects from a Video

Once you've added text effects, transitions, or visual effects to your video, you can remove them at any time. To remove effects or transitions, follow these steps:

1. Right-click the effect or transition you want to remove. A pop-up menu appears.

2. Click **Delete**. (If you want to delete all effects or transitions, click **Delete All Transitions**, **Delete All Video Effects**, or **Delete All Text Effects**.) Nero removes your chosen transition or effect.

Saving a NeroVision Project

Once you've trimmed your video and added transitions or visual and text effects, you may want to save your project so you can burn it to a CD or DVD later. To save a NeroVision project, follow these steps:

1. Click the **Save** button. If you have previously saved your NeroVision project, Nero just saves it again. If this is the first time you are saving this project, Nero displays a Save As dialog box.

2. Type a descriptive name for your project. (You may also want to change the drive or folder where you store your project.)

3. Click **Save**.

Exporting Part of a Video

Rather than save your entire video file as a NeroVision project, you can also export all or part of your video file to a separate video file, which you can later load into a separate program, send to someone through email, burn to a CD or DVD, or transfer back to a digital video camera.

To export a video, follow these steps:

1. Start the StartSmart menu.

2. Click the **Standard Mode** button to display the expert mode options.

3. Click the **Photo and Video** category.

4. Click **Make Movie**. The NeroVision Express window appears and displays the last project you worked on.

5. (Optional.) Click **Next** if you want to load a new project, and then click **Open Saved Project or Disc Image**. When an Open dialog box appears, click the project you want to edit, and click **Open**. Nero displays your chosen project.

6. Click the **Storyboard** tab. Nero displays the Storyboard view.

7. In the Storyboard view, click the part of your video that you want to export. Nero displays a blue border around your selected video.

8. Click the **Export** button. An Export Video window appears, as shown in Figure 11-13.

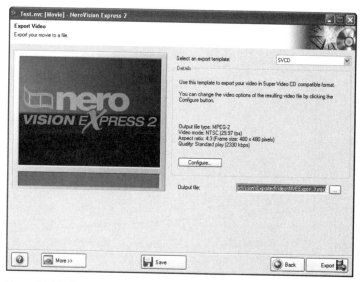

Figure 11-13: The Export Video window gives you options for saving your video as a separate file

9. Click in the **Select an export template** list box, and choose one of the following options:

    SVCD   Saves your file for later burning as a Super VCD

    VCD   Saves your file for later burning as a VCD

    Custom   Lets you define the settings for saving your file in different file formats, such as MPEG-2 or AVI

    DV   Saves your video for transferring to a digital video camera

    E-Mail   Saves your video as a small, compressed file suitable for sending by email

10. Click the **Output file** button (the button with three dots on it). A Select a Location for the Video File dialog box appears.

11. Type a name for your exported video file. (You may also want to specify the drive and folder where you want to save your exported video file.)

12. Click **Save**.

13. Click **Export**. Nero exports your chosen video. This process may take a few minutes, depending on how long your video is.

12

USING THE NERO TOOLKIT

Despite all the fancy technical specifications that most computers come with, most people quickly forget what type of equipment their computer might have and what it can do for them. To help you identify and tweak your CD and DVD drives for optimum playback and burning performance, Nero comes with a handful of tools to probe your computer and show you exactly what your CD and DVD drives are capable of doing. Nero's toolkit programs aren't something you're likely to use every day, but you'll be happy to have them around when you need them.

Probing Your Computer with Nero InfoTool

Nero InfoTool can tell you a variety of things about your computer that can be useful for troubleshooting or learning what types of CDs or DVDs your computer may be capable of reading from and writing to.

These are some of the things that Nero InfoTool can reveal:

- **Software** What operating system version your computer uses, what version of the DirectX graphics library you have installed, and the exact version numbers of all the different Nero programs on your computer (see Figure 12-1). To make sure you have the latest version of the different Nero programs, refer to the appendix to learn how to update your Nero programs over the Internet.

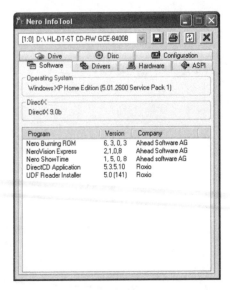

Figure 12-1: The Software tab shows the version numbers of all your Nero programs

- **Drivers** The names and version numbers of the various drivers, video codecs, and audio codecs installed on your computer (see Figure 12-2). Codecs (which stands for compression/decompression) are programs, developed by different companies, that Nero uses to compress and read video and audio files.

- **Hardware** The video and sound controllers, the BIOS type and version number, the processor type and speed, the motherboard name, and the amount of RAM your computer has installed (see Figure 12-3).

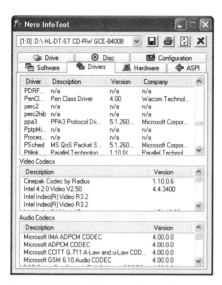

Figure 12-2: The Drivers tab lists the names and versions of all the drivers that keep your computer working (hopefully)

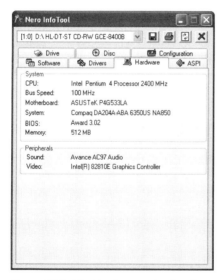

Figure 12-3: The Hardware tab identifies your processor type and speed, and the video and sound controllers

- **ASPI** The names and version numbers of the various files installed for your computer's ASPI (Advanced SCSI Programming Interface) installation, which is software that controls all the SCSI devices on your computer (see Figure 12-4 on the next page).

Drive
list box

Figure 12-4: The ASPI tab shows the names and version numbers of all the files used in your ASPI installation

- **Drive**   The read and write capabilities of the CD or DVD drive currently displayed in the Drive list box (see Figure 12-5). Such capabilities include the exact types of CD or DVD discs your drive can recognize, its maximum read and write speeds, and whether the drive supports buffer underrun protection.

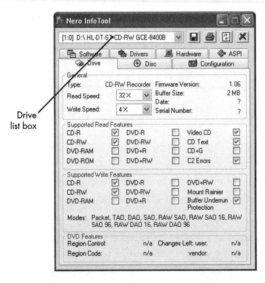

Drive
list box

Figure 12-5: The Drive tab identifies the specific features of the CD or DVD drive currently displayed in the Drive list box

- **Disc** The capacity and content of the CD or DVD currently displayed in the Drive list box (see Figure 12-6). Within the Extended Information group, you can see how many tracks (files) the disc may contain along with the number of times it has been written to (referred to as "sessions"). If you insert a new disc in your drive, click the **Refresh** button so Nero can identify the new disc.

Figure 12-6: The Disc tab lists the specific capabilities of the CD or DVD currently inside a particular CD or DVD drive

- **Configuration** The name and type of CD, DVD, and hard drives connected to your computer (see Figure 12-7).

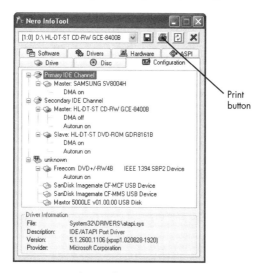

Figure 12-7: The Configuration tab lists all the CD, DVD, and hard drives attached to your computer

To run Nero InfoTool, follow these steps:

1. Start the StartSmart menu.
2. Click the **Extras** category.
3. Click **Get System Info**. The Nero InfoTool window appears.
4. Click a tab, such as **Disc** or **Hardware**, to display specific information about your computer, such as the drivers or operating system version installed.
5. (Optional.) Click the **Print** button to print out the information currently displayed.

Testing Your CDs and DVDs

Despite all the marketing hype, not all CD and DVD drives and discs are equal. If you're having trouble writing to a disc or reading data stored on a CD or DVD, or you just want to compare different disc brands to find the one that works best in your drive, you can use Nero CD-DVD Speed to examine the physical quality of your CDs or DVDs and the capabilities of your CD and DVD drives.

To run Nero CD-DVD Speed, follow these steps:

1. Start the StartSmart menu.
2. Click the **Extras** category.
3. Click **Test Drive**. The Nero CD-DVD Speed window appears.

Nero CD-DVD Speed can check your CD/DVDs for quality, surface flaws, and support for *overburning*, which is the ability to store more data than normal. (Overburning can often cram more data on a CD, but with the possible drawback that the disc won't be usable in another computer.)

NOTE *It's perfectly possible to have a CD or DVD that your computer can read perfectly, but that isn't readable by any other computer or CD/DVD player. The more errors Nero detects on a disc, the more likely that the disc may have problems working on another computer or CD/DVD player. When Nero detects errors, the problem could be either a defective disc or a defective CD or DVD drive.*

Performing a CD Quality Check

Before wasting your time trying to burn music or data files to a CD, you may want to run a quality check on the CD to make sure the disc will be usable.

NOTE *The following steps can only test the quality of CDs, not DVDs.*

To check a CD, follow these steps:

1. Run Nero CD-DVD Speed by following the steps in the earlier "Testing Your CDs and DVDs" section.

2. Insert the CD that you want to test into your CD or DVD drive.

3. Click the **drive** list box and choose the CD or DVD drive into which you inserted your CD.

4. Click the **Extra** menu and click **CD quality test**. A CD Speed dialog box appears. Figure 12-8 shows two CD Speed dialog boxes: the first shows a disc with errors on it, and the second shows a disc with no errors.

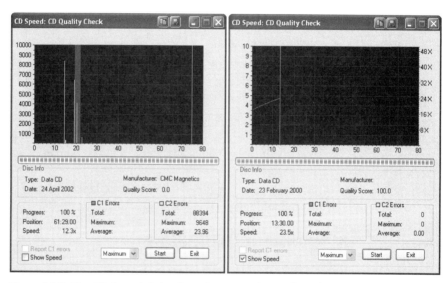

Figure 12-8: The CD Speed dialog box shows you the number of errors on your CD

5. Click the **Start** button. Nero CD-DVD Speed displays the results of its analysis of your disc.

6. Click **Exit** when you're finished.

Many CDs have errors, so don't be surprised to find a few on your discs, especially if they've been heavily used. C1 errors are often minor problems that occur when reading a disc. C2 errors can be more serious and may indicate the presence of scratches or other surface defects.

If you find a rewritable disc (such as a CD+RW or DVD+RW disc) with a large number of errors, you can often fix the disc by copying any important data off it and then erasing the entire disc. (This method won't work with CD-R or DVD-R discs that cannot be erased.)

Scanning the Surface of a Disc

Sometimes disc errors can occur because of slight imperfections in different CD or DVD drives, so while one drive may have no trouble reading a disc, another drive may refuse to recognize it entirely. If you suspect that the problem with reading a disc is caused by scratches or imperfections on the disc itself, you can run a surface scan to check the physical quality of the disc.

To scan the surface of a CD/DVD, follow these steps:

1. Run Nero CD-DVD Speed by following the steps in the earlier "Testing Your CDs and DVDs" section.

2. Insert the CD/DVD that you want to scan into your CD or DVD drive.

3. Click the **drive** list box and choose the CD or DVD drive into which you inserted your CD.

4. Click the **Extra** menu and click **ScanDisc**. A ScanDisc dialog box appears.

5. (Optional.) Click in the **File text** check box if you want to examine any files stored on your CD/DVD.

6. Click in the **Surface Scan** check box.

7. Click **Start**. The ScanDisc dialog box displays the surface of your CD/DVD in color codes to show you good, damaged, and unreadable parts of your disc, as shown in Figure 12-9.

8. Click **Close** when you're finished. (If a CD/DVD is too badly damaged or is unreadable, you can always recycle it as a coaster.)

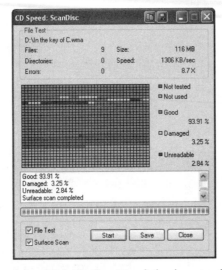

Figure 12-9: The ScanDisc dialog box visually shows you how much of your CD/DVD may be damaged or unreadable

Checking a Disc's Transfer Rate

The transfer rate is how fast your drive can read data from a disc. A disc may be perfectly readable but could contain defects that force your drive to reread some data, thus slowing down the transfer rate.

To test your disc's transfer rate with your drive, follow these steps:

1. Run Nero CD-DVD Speed by following the steps in the earlier "Testing Your CDs and DVDs" section.

2. Insert the CD/DVD that you want to scan into your CD or DVD drive.

3. Click the **drive** list box and choose the CD or DVD drive into which you inserted your CD.

4. Click the **Run Test** menu and click **Transfer Rate** (or press **F2**). Nero CD-DVD Speed displays the results of the transfer rate test, as shown in Figure 12-10.

The green line shows the transfer rate, the yellow line shows the rotation speed, and the red vertical line shows the amount of data stored on your disc. If you see large dips in the green or yellow lines, your drive had to reread parts of your disc to retrieve the data, slowing down the transfer rate. Such slowdowns could indicate problems with the disc, such as scratches or just the overall poor quality of the disc.

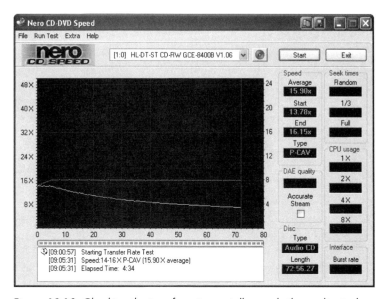

Figure 12-10: Checking the transfer rate can tell you whether a disc is damaged or made poorly

Testing Your CD and DVD Drives

Besides the quality of your discs, the second major factor in burning CDs is the quality of your rewritable CD and DVD drives. While most CD and DVD drives are reliable, there can be major differences between brands and models. Nero provides a set of handy tests you can run to see how well your particular CD and DVD drives really work.

NOTE *This whole section is about testing the drives, not the CD or DVD discs themselves. You can use DVD discs for some of these tests but other tests may only work with CD. In general, as long as your drive works and lets you burn CDs or DVDs, most people won't care about how fast their drive accesses data off a CD, but technically minded users may still want to peek at their drive's capabilities just for the fun of it.*

Running a Digital Audio Extraction (DAE) Quality Test

One of the most popular uses for a CD or DVD drive is to copy or "rip" audio tracks from a commercial audio CD and save them in another digital audio file format. To test how efficient your CD or DVD drives are at ripping audio tracks from a CD, you can run a Digital Audio Extraction (DAE) test.

This test first copies some audio sectors from three different places on an audio CD and stores them on your hard disk. Then Nero reads those sectors from your audio CD again to compare them with the versions stored on your hard disk. After comparing the two, Nero rates your CD or DVD drive from 0 to 10, where 10 means a perfect DAE (no differences between the two versions).

In addition, Nero also checks to see whether your drive supports *accurate streaming,* which can speed up the ripping process. Accurate streaming can be important, because CDs don't store audio data sequentially on the surface of a disc. That way, if the disc gets scratched, that single scratch won't tear out a huge chunk of a song. Instead of storing audio data sequentially, CDs interleave audio data in different parts of the disc.

While scattering audio data around ensures that a single scratch won't wreck an entire song, it does force your drive to spend extra time searching for all the data that makes up an audio file. A drive that supports accurate streaming can search for audio data quickly, and a drive that doesn't support accurate streaming will take longer to rip audio tracks from a CD.

To run a DAE test, follow these steps:

1. Run Nero CD-DVD Speed by following the steps in the earlier "Testing Your CDs and DVDs" section.
2. Insert an audio CD in a CD or DVD drive.
3. Click the **drive** list box and choose the CD or DVD drive in which you inserted your CD.
4. Click the **Extra** menu and click **DAE Quality** (or press **F3**). Nero displays the results for your drive, as shown in Figure 12-11.

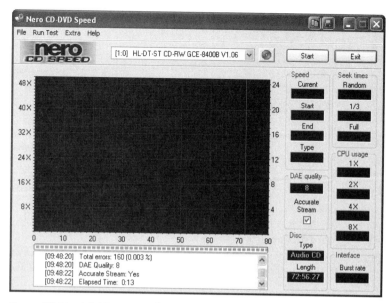

Figure 12-11: A DAE test can determine how well your drive can rip audio tracks from a disc

Testing a Drive for Overburning Capabilities

With some CD and DVD drives, it's actually possible to burn more data onto a CD than is advertised as its storage capacity — a process called *overburning*. Just be aware that an overburned CD may not be readable by another computer. To check whether your CD or DVD drive allows for overburning and how much data you might be able to cram onto a CD, follow these steps:

1. Run Nero CD-DVD Speed by following the steps in the earlier "Testing Your CDs and DVDs" section.

2. Insert a blank, rewritable CD+RW disc in your rewritable CD or DVD drive.

3. Click the **drive** list box and choose the rewritable CD or DVD drive in which you inserted your CD.

4. Click the **Extra** menu and click **Overburning test**. An Overburning Test dialog box appears, as shown in Figure 12-12 on the next page. (If the Start button in the dialog box appears dimmed, the CD or DVD drive you selected does not support overburning.)

5. Click in the **Write Speed** list box and choose a speed, such as **4x**.

6. Click the **Start** button. When Nero CD-DVD Speed is done testing, it displays the stated capacity of the CD, the extra amount of data that overburning could add, and the total maximum storage capacity of the disk if you use overburning.

Figure 12-12: The Overburning Test dialog box can tell you whether your rewritable CD or DVD drive supports overburning and how much extra data you can burn onto a CD

Measuring Drive Seek Times

The seek-time test measures how quickly your drive can move to random spots on a disc, from the beginning of your disc to a new position one-third of the way into the disc, and from the beginning to the end of a disc. To measure the seek time, follow these steps:

1. Run Nero CD-DVD Speed by following the steps in the earlier "Testing Your CDs and DVDs" section.

2. Insert a disc into your rewritable CD or DVD drive.

3. Click the **drive** list box and choose the CD or DVD drive into which you inserted your disc.

4. Click the **Run Test** menu and click **Access/Seek times** (or press **F4**). Nero CD-DVD Speed displays the results of the access- and seek-time test, as shown in Figure 12-13.

Measuring CPU Usage at Different Speeds

In case you want to know how different drive speeds affect your computer's CPU (central processing unit), you can run a CPU usage test by following these steps:

1. Run Nero CD-DVD Speed by following the steps in the earlier "Testing Your CDs and DVDs" section.

2. Insert a disc into your rewritable CD or DVD drive.

3. Click the **drive** list box and choose the CD or DVD drive in which you inserted your disc.

4. Click the **Run Test** menu and click **CPU Usage** (or press **F5**). Nero CD-DVD Speed displays the results of the CPU usage test, showing by what percentage different drive speeds affect your CPU.

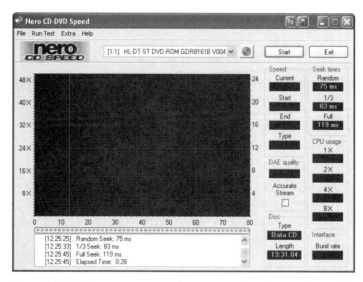

Figure 12-13: Nero can measure the access and seek times of your drive

Determining a CD or DVD Drive's Burst Rate

The burst-rate test measures the transfer rate from the host adapter to your CD or DVD drive.

To run the burst-rate test, follow these steps:

1. Run Nero CD-DVD Speed by following the steps in the earlier "Testing Your CDs and DVDs" section.
2. Insert a disc into your rewritable CD or DVD drive.
3. Click the **drive** list box and choose the CD or DVD drive in which you inserted your disc.
4. Click the **Run Test** menu and click **Burst Rate** (or press **F6**). Nero CD-DVD Speed displays the burst rate of your CD or DVD drive.

Measuring Spin-Up and Spin-Down Times

The faster your drive is, the less time it will take to spin up and start reading data and then to spin down afterward. To run the spin-up and spin-down test, follow these steps:

1. Run Nero CD-DVD Speed by following the steps in the earlier "Testing Your CDs and DVDs" section.
2. Insert a disc into your rewritable CD or DVD drive.

3. Click the **drive** list box and choose the CD or DVD drive in which you inserted your disc.

4. Click the **Run Test** menu and click **Spin Up/Down** (or press **F7**). Nero CD-DVD Speed displays the spin-up and spin-down times for your chosen drive.

Measuring Load and Eject Times

The load- and eject-time test measures how quickly your drive can eject and load a disc. To run this test, follow these steps:

1. Run Nero CD-DVD Speed by following the steps in the earlier "Testing Your CDs and DVDs" section.

2. Insert a disc into your rewritable CD or DVD drive.

3. Click the **drive** list box and choose the CD or DVD drive in which you inserted your disc.

4. Click the **Run Test** menu and click **Load/Eject** (or press **F8**). Nero CD-DVD Speed displays the times for loading and ejecting a disc.

Manipulating the Speed of Your Drives

For maximum control, Nero lets you control the speed of your individual CD or DVD drives. While you may normally want your drives running at the fastest speed possible, you might want to slow down your drives for several reasons:

- **Noise** High-speed drives can make an irritating whine, which can be especially distracting if you're trying to listen to music from an audio CD. Generally, a reading speed of 4x is more than adequate for playing digital audio files from a disc.

- **Spin-up and spin-down times** High-speed drives take more time to spin up and down, which means you may have to wait if your drive needs to read additional data from a disc. This can be annoying when playing a game from a CD, because every time the game needs additional data, your game may slow or pause while your drive spins up to retrieve the necessary data.

- **Reading damaged discs** Every time your drive comes across a disc error, it slows down and tries to read the data again. Forcing your drive to speed up and then slow down again when encountering errors on heavily damaged discs can physically damage your drives. By slowing down your drive, you can prevent this additional wear from occurring.

To modify the speed of your drive, follow these steps:

1. Start the StartSmart menu.
2. Click the **Extras** category.
3. Click **Control Drive's Speed**. The Nero DriveSpeed dialog box appears, as shown in Figure 12-14.

Figure 12-14: Nero lets you change the read and spin-down speeds of your CD/DVD drives

4. Click in the **drive** list box and choose the drive that you want to modify.
5. Click in the **CD Read Speed** list box and choose a speed, such as **24X**.
6. Click in the **DVD Read Speed** list box and choose a speed.
7. Click in the **Spin Down Time** list box and choose a time, such as **32 sec**.
8. Click in one or more of the following check boxes:

    Run at startup   Makes your CD and DVD drives run at the settings you defined whenever you turn on your computer.

    Start minimized   Keeps the Nero DriveSpeed dialog box minimized if you choose to run Nero DriveSpeed at startup.

    Restore speed settings at startup   Abandons any speed settings you may have defined for your CD or DVD drives each time you restart your computer.

9. Click **Close**.

A

INSTALLING, UPDATING, AND UNINSTALLING NERO

Before you can use Nero, you have to install it. And then you should update your copy of Nero before you start playing around with it, so you have the newest features and the latest bug fixes to make Nero work perfectly on your computer. And finally, if you don't like or need certain parts of Nero, you can always uninstall one or more of the different programs.

Installing Nero

When you install Nero, you can choose which programs you want to install. That means you can just install the parts of Nero that you really need, such as its CD-burning program, and skip the programs you might not need at this time, like the DVD-burning program.

To install Nero, follow these steps:

1. Insert the Nero CD into your computer. (If the Nero installation window doesn't appear, follow steps 2 through 6. Otherwise, skip to step 7.)
2. Click the **Start** button and then click **Run**. A Run dialog box appears.
3. Click the **Browse** button. A Browse dialog box appears.
4. Click the **Look in** list box and choose the drive where you put the Nero CD. A bunch of Nero folders appear in the **Browse** dialog box, as shown in Figure A-1.

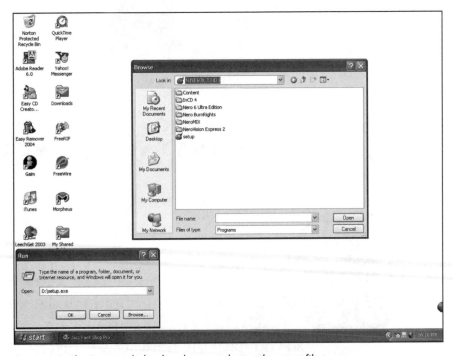

Figure A-1: The Browse dialog box lets you choose the setup file to run

5. Double-click the **setup** icon (or click the **setup** icon once and then click the **Open** button). The setup.exe filename appears in the Run dialog box.
6. Click **OK**. The Nero Installer dialog box appears, as shown in Figure A-2. The installation program lets you choose which parts of Nero you want to install, such as NeroMix or Nero 6 Ultra Edition.
7. Click one of the Nero programs you want to install, such as **Nero 6 Ultra Edition**. (When you get done installing one of the Nero programs, the Nero Installer dialog box pops up again so you can install another Nero program if you want.)

Figure A-2: The Nero Installer dialog box lets you choose the Nero program you want to install

8. Follow the instructions that appear in the dialog box. (The first time you install any of the Nero programs, you'll need to type in your Nero serial number. Once you type in this serial number once, you won't have to type it in to install any of the other Nero programs.) When you're finished, the Nero Installer dialog box reappears to let you install another Nero program.

9. Repeat steps 7 and 8 for each Nero program you want to install. Or click the **Exit** button to quit installing Nero programs.

Updating Your Copy of Nero

The version of Nero that you received on your Nero installation CD most likely isn't the latest version. Once you've installed Nero, take a few moments to update your copy with the latest bug fixes and program features. Updating Nero requires an Internet connection (the faster, the better). If you don't have an Internet connection, you can ignore this section.

Checking Your Nero Version Numbers

Every Nero program includes a version number. You can view version numbers individually by starting up each program, clicking the **Help** menu, and then clicking **About**, but it's much faster to view all your program version numbers from the StartSmart menu at once. Not only can the StartSmart menu show you the version number of each program, but it can also show you the latest versions available for each program.

Updating Nero with the StartSmart Menu

To see the version numbers of your Nero programs and update them, follow
these steps:

1. Connect to the Internet.
2. Start the StartSmart menu.
3. Click the **Nero ProductCenter** button. The StartSmart menu displays all
    the Nero programs installed on your computer, along with the latest ver-
    sions available, as shown in Figure A-3.

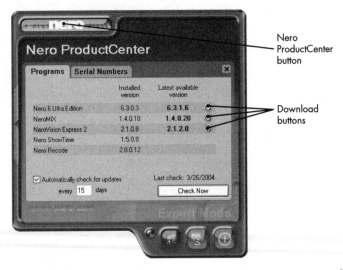

*Figure A-3: The StartSmart menu can show you the current versions of your installed
Nero programs*

4. Click the **Check Now** button. Nero connects to the Nero Web site to
    determine whether there are newer versions of your Nero programs
    available. If Nero finds a newer version of a program, it lists the latest
    version number and displays a green Download button next to it.
5. Click the **Download** button for each program that you want to update.
6. Nero opens your Web browser and displays the Nero Web page, where
    you can download your chosen program updates.
7. Follow steps 6 through 13 in the "Updating Nero manually" section
    that follows.
8. Click the close box to remove the Nero ProductCenter dialog box from
    the StartSmart menu.

Updating Nero Manually

To update Nero without going through the StartSmart menu, follow
these steps:

1. Connect to the Internet using your favorite browser.
2. Go to www.nero.com to view the Nero Web site.
3. Click **Downloads**.
4. Click **Updates**. A list of program updates appears directly under the Updates link.
5. Click **Updates Nero 6**. The Nero Web site lists several updates you can download to update different Nero programs, as shown in Figure A-4. (You may have to scroll down this Web page to see the Nero program updates.)

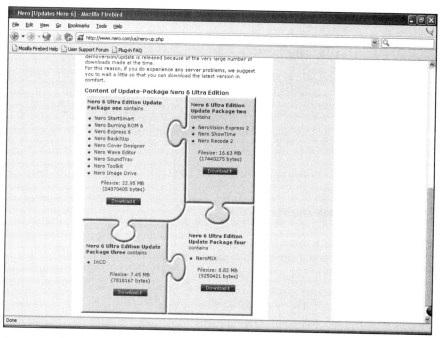

Figure A-4: The Nero Web site gives you the option of downloading different files to update the various Nero programs

6. Click the **Download It** button for the Nero update you want. A dialog box pops up, asking you where you want to save your chosen Nero update.
7. Select the folder where you want to store your Nero update, and then click **OK**. (Don't forget which folder you chose!)
8. Click the **Start** button and click **Run**. A Run dialog box appears.
9. Click the **Browse** button. A Browse dialog box appears.
10. Click the folder where you stored the Nero update file in step 7.
11. Double-click the Nero update file, which may have a cryptic name, such as nero6303.exe.

12. Click **OK** in the Run dialog box to run the Nero update program. Nero displays a dialog box as it updates your copy of Nero, as shown in Figure A-5.

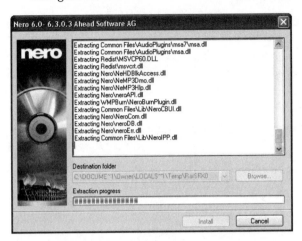

Figure A-5: The Nero update file can automatically update your copy of Nero right before your eyes

13. Follow the onscreen instructions to update your copy of Nero.

Uninstalling Nero

If for some reason you no longer want Nero on your hard disk, you can always uninstall it. Uninstalling Nero simply removes every single trace of the Nero program from your hard disk. What uninstalling won't do, however, is remove any folders or files you may have created when using Nero, such as MP3 files or CD label designs.

NOTE *When you uninstall Nero, you can selectively choose which parts of the Nero program you want to remove. It's possible to keep Nero's CD-burning program and just get rid of Nero's audio player program, for example.*

To uninstall a Nero program, follow these steps:

1. Click the **Start** button and click **Control Panel**. (If you're running an older version of Windows, such as Windows 2000, click the **Start** button, click **Settings**, and then click **Control Panel**.) The Control Panel window appears.

2. Double-click the **Add or Remove Programs** icon. (Windows 2000 and other versions of Windows have an **Add/Remove Programs** icon instead.) The Add or Remove Programs window appears.

3. Click the Nero program you wish to uninstall, such as **Nero 6 Ultra Edition**, **NeroMix**, or **NeroVision Express 2**, as shown in Figure A-6. (You may have to scroll down through a long list of programs already installed on your computer.)

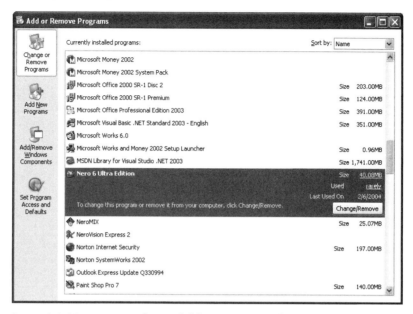

Figure A-6: Nero consists of several different programs that you can uninstall individually

4. Click the **Change/Remove** button. A dialog box guides you through the rest of the uninstallation process. Just follow the instructions, which usually means simply clicking a button to continue uninstalling your chosen program. Uninstalling may take a few minutes, depending on the speed of your machine.

INDEX

STEAL THIS FILE SHARING BOOK

What They Won't Tell You About File Sharing

by WALLACE WANG *&* JERRY BULLFROG

SEPTEMBER 2004, 392 PP.
$19.95, $27.95 CAN
ISBN 1-59327-050-X

Steal This File Sharing Book peels back the mystery surrounding file-sharing networks such as Kazaa, Morpheus, and Usenet, showing you how they work and how to use them wisely. It reveals the dangers of using file-sharing networks — including viruses, spyware, and lawsuits — and tells you how to avoid them. Includes coverage of the ongoing battle between the software, video, and music pirates and the industries that are trying to stop them.

THE SPAM LETTERS

by JONATHAN LAND

JUNE 2004, 232 PP.
$14.95, $19.95 CAN
ISBN 1-59327-032-1

From the man behind TheSpamLetters.com — featured in *Entertainment Weekly, The New York Times,* and Slashdot — comes a collection of brilliant and entertaining correspondence with the people who send out mass junk emailings (a.k.a. spam). Compiled from the nearly 200 entries written by Jonathan Land, *The Spam Letters* taunts, prods, and parodies the faceless salespeople in your inbox, giving you a chuckle at their expense. If you hate spam, you'll love *The Spam Letters.*

STEAL THIS COMPUTER BOOK 3

What They Won't Tell You About the Internet

by WALLACE WANG

2003, 384 PP.
$24.95, $37.95 CAN
ISBN 1-59327-000-3

This offbeat, non-technical book looks at what hackers do, how they do it, and how you can protect yourself. The third edition of this bestseller (over 150,000 copies sold) is updated to cover rootkits, spyware, web bugs, identity theft, hacktivism, wireless hacking (wardriving), biometrics, and firewalls.

THE CULT OF MAC

by LEANDER KAHNEY

SEPTEMBER 2004, 376 PP., HARDCOVER, 4-COLOR
$39.95, $55.95 CAN
ISBN 1-886411-83-2

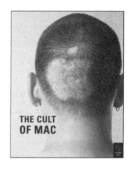

There is no product on the planet that enjoys the devotion of a Macintosh computer. Apple's machines have legions of loyal, sometimes demented fans. *The Cult of Mac* surveys the devoted following that has grown up around Macintosh computers. From people who get Mac tattoos and haircuts, to those who furnish their apartments out of Macintosh computer boxes, this full-color coffee table book details Mac fanaticism in all of its forms.

"If you want to understand what we did, why we did it, and how it worked (or didn't), this is the book to read. It's required reading for anyone who loves his or her Macintosh." — Guy Kawasaki, Mac Evangelist and author of *The Art of the Start*

APPLE CONFIDENTIAL 2.0
The Definitive History of the World's Most Colorful Company

by OWEN W. LINZMAYER

JANUARY 2004, 344 PP.
$19.95, $29.95 CAN
ISBN 1-59327-010-0

Apple Confidential examines the tumultuous history of America's best-known Silicon Valley start-up — from its legendary founding almost 30 years ago, through a series of disastrous executive decisions, to its return to profitability, and including Apple's recent move into the music business. This updated and expanded edition includes tons of new photos, timelines, and charts, as well as coverage of new lawsuit battles, updates on former Apple executives, and new chapters on Steve Wozniak and Pixar.

"If you're a member of the Mac faithful or just moderately interested in the company, you simply must buy this book." — macdevcenter.com

PHONE:
1 (800) 420-7240 OR
(415) 863-9900
MONDAY THROUGH FRIDAY,
9 A.M. TO 5 P.M. (PST)

FAX:
(415) 863-9950
24 HOURS A DAY,
7 DAYS A WEEK

EMAIL:
SALES@NOSTARCH.COM

WEB:
HTTP://WWW.NOSTARCH.COM

MAIL:
NO STARCH PRESS
555 DE HARO ST, SUITE 250
SAN FRANCISCO, CA 94107
USA

UPDATES

Visit **http://www.nostarch.com/nero.htm** for updates, errata, and other information.